THE SATURDAY EVENING POST

Family Cookbook

COLLECTOR'S EDITION

The Curtis Publishing Company
Indianapolis, Indiana

CONTENTS

One of the wonderful things about cooking is that it is creative. It is an art and will always remain so.

This is not to belittle the computerized wonders of packaged and frozen foods. But the true medium of cooking is first the marketplace where decisions are made; then the planning, for the little touches that create excitement and harmony at the table; and finally the intuitive processes of cooking, which are not matters of measurement but of experience and imagination. Is a soufflé ready to come out? Only the eye can answer. Is the meat just the right degree of rareness, between raw and overdone, deep down in the center of the roast or steak? Only the instinct of the cook can be the judge. The kind of cook who has studied the marbleization of the meat beforehand and senses whether it will broil or roast moist or dry.

Such culinary art lurks in the kitchens of a thousand farmhouses, in the little black books tucked in the top drawers of a thousand kitchens, and even more remotely, in the recesses of the minds of countless numbers who love to cook. Many and great are the cookbooks which have been written in the past, but still there is the suspicion that the best is yet to come, if ever it could be pried from its myriad hiding places in homes where a recipe means "eat" instead of "publish."

Reflecting on these things, the editors of *The Saturday Evening Post* decided to announce a recipe contest and to call on the households of America for their most treasured dishes. The *Post Family Cookbook* contains a selection of these recipes, some of them recipes which have been passed on lovingly from generation to generation. Because the *Post* is regarded as something akin to a family friend, there was a willingness on the part of *Post* cooks to share the secrets of favorite dishes.

Thank you, *Post* readers. Thank you for telling us about Maple Blueberry Cake and Lasagne Verde, Sweet-Sour Shrimp and Eggplant aux Champignons, Grape-Apple Crumble and Mai Tai Mousse. Thank you for helping to make this most varied and out-of-the-ordinary collection of recipes ever published under the *Post* name.

To round out the cookbook we have included some classic recipes that appeared in the magazine in years gone by, new recipes from the kitchens of famous friends, and an assortment of great *Post* cartoons.

Laughter is the magic seasoning that can make good food taste even better. So enjoy! Enjoy!

The Editors of The Saturday Evening Post

SALADS

The Sharing of the Green

"One order 'Chef's Salad.'"

8

RICHARD NIXON'S AVOCADO SALAD

Mash 2 medium-sized avocados. Stir into slightly thickened lemon Jell-O base made with

1 package lemon Jell-O
3 tablespoons lemon juice
1½ cups hot water

Stir in 1 can (#2) of grapefruit sections drained, and ½ cup chopped celery. Chill and unmold. Serve with a whipped cream and mayonnaise mixture.

LADY BIRD JOHNSON'S
MOLDED CRANBERRY SALAD

Part of the Johnson family tradition is this salad, served for holidays with chicken or turkey.

1 envelope unflavored
  gelatin
1¼ cups cold water
1 cup sugar
2 cups cranberries

½ cup chopped celery
½ cup chopped nuts (pecans
  are excellent)
½ teaspoon salt

Cook cranberries in 1 cup water for 20 minutes. Stir in sugar and cook 5 minutes longer. Soften gelatin in ¼ cup cold water; add to hot cranberries and stir until dissolved. Set aside to cool. When mixture begins to thicken, add chopped celery, nuts and salt. Turn into mold that has been rinsed with cold water. Chill in refrigerator until firm. Unmold on serving plate. Garnish with salad greens if desired. Makes about 6 servings.

CLARE BOOTHE LUCE'S
GOLDEN DOLPHIN SALAD

I never can quite make up my mind whether I prefer a Chef's Salad or a Caesar Salad. My cook, Katherine Yokoyama, surprised me by combining the ingredients of both—with an Oriental touch of her own—cutting them up into non-lipstick-smearing bite sizes. So I named the salad The Golden Dolphin after my Honolulu house. It's not only my favorite salad, but everyone else's who eats it.

1 small head iceberg lettuce
2 small heads butter lettuce
½ head romaine
¾ bunch watercress
1 small cucumber, peeled
  and diced thinly

4 slices cooked ham, diced
3 slices Swiss cheese, diced
¼ cup fresh grated Parmesan
1 small can anchovies, in 1-inch slices
½ cup croutons, toasted in
  garlic butter

Cut all greens into ½-inch lengths. Toss the above ingredients (except the croutons) lightly with the following dressing:

1/3 cup white wine vinegar
2/3 cup olive oil
Dash Worcestershire sauce
2 garlic buds—put through press

¼ teaspoon salad herbs
Dash Ajinamoto or Accent
Salt, pepper to taste

Before serving, add toasted croutons, one well-beaten raw egg. Toss lightly.

DICK VAN DYKE'S POOR RICHARD'S SALAD

This salad was given to Dick by a friend named Richard shortly after Dick was married. It's been a favorite and a filler ever since.

1 package beef wieners chopped
  into bite size
½ box Velveeta cheese
1 medium-sized jar
  gherkin pickles

4 stalks celery
10 scallions
1 small can, drained, peas
1 package cooked macaroni shells

Mix together, add salad herbs, ¼ cup pickle juice and lots of mayonnaise. Serve cold. A perfect picnic salad.

LUCILLE BALL'S FAVORITE SALAD

My favorite salad is one I can make in a hurry, because that's the way I do almost everything. I call it a "Tropical Treat," although I'm sure that's probably not its real name. I think the first time I tasted it was in Hawaii, but I remembered the ingredients because everyone I have served it to since has always enjoyed it. It can also serve as a dessert if you don't want to stuff your guests.

I make it in individual salad bowls, which you may or may not chill before assembling your ingredients. They consist of thinly sliced bananas, pineapple rings, finely chopped nuts, lettuce and a dressing of mayonnaise and half-and-half. After that, it's simple. Line the bottom of the bowl with crisp lettuce leaves, lay in several pineapple rings, then a layer of sliced bananas. Prepare the dressing ahead of time by combining the half-and-half with mayonnaise and stirring into a thick, creamy mixture. Spoon the dressing over the salad, sprinkle with chopped nuts, and top it with a cherry.

I usually serve this with a menu of thinly sliced steak and scalloped potatoes. It's also good with a meat casserole.

BILLY GRAHAM'S POPPY SEED DRESSING

Mix:
1½ cups sugar
2 teaspoons dry mustard

2 teaspoons salt
2/3 cup vinegar

Add and stir thoroughly 3 tablespoons onion juice. Slowly add, beating constantly, 2 cups Mazola oil. Continue beating until thick. Stir in 2 tablespoons poppy seeds to taste. Store in refrigerator. Makes 3 1/3 cups.

9

ISAAC ASIMOV'S
BEAN SALAD VARIEE

10

Combine kidney beans, cooked and drained, minced green onions (to taste), cabbage, preferably purple—small amount, finely shredded. A small carrot, grated, *pignoli* or sesame seeds, green pepper, small, minced. Salt and coarsely ground pepper. Add a dressing of mayonnaise plus mustard, curry powder and a little lemon juice. Mix and put on a bed of greens (endive and Boston lettuce). Add some cherry tomatoes and more dressing to top. For variety, add crumbled bacon, or tuna fish, or chopped artichoke hearts, or sautéed mushrooms. Or use horseradish instead of curry with mayonnaise.

YOUSUF KARSH'S
FAVORITE SALADS

Yousuf Karsh, the great Canadian photographer, has sculpted the world's leaders with his camera. His famous portraits of Churchill, Albert Schweitzer and Einstein live in our minds as vividly as the great men themselves. Mardin is the name of the town in Armenia where he was born. Recently, he returned from Holland, where he photographed HRH Prince Bernhard, and England where he made portraits of the great sculptor, Henry Moore.

ENDIVE AND WATERCRESS SALAD

Although this is one of the simplest salads, Karsh reports it is sheer delight to the palate. It is delicate enough to accompany the entree, but it should not be eaten all at once beforehand. Gently separate the leaves of the endive—do not chip, bruise, or cut them. Add sprigs of delicate watercress. For the dressing, simply squeeze over the salad the juice of half a lemon. Fresh lemon juice, alone is Karsh's preference for a dressing.

MARDIN SALAD

1 large onion
3 small cucumbers
5 medium-sized tomatoes
1 green pepper
About ¼ cup salad oil

Lemon juice (the juice from
  1½ lemons is suggested)
Parsley
Salt—to taste.

Cube all ingredients, small size, and finely chop the parsley.

SOUR CREAM PINA-BERRY SALAD

1 (3-ounce) package
  strawberry-flavored gelatin
1 cup boiling water,
  minus 1 tablespoon
1 cup pineapple juice,
  minus 1 tablespoon

1 (8¼-ounce) can crushed pineapple,
  well drained
1 cup commercial sour cream
1 (10-ounce) package frozen
  sweetened strawberry halves,
  thawed and well drained

Pour boiling water over gelatin and stir until dissolved. Add pineapple juice and blend well. Pour half of mixture into an 8-inch square pan. Refrigerate. Leave other half of gelatin at room temperature. As soon as gelatin in refrigerator is partially set (about 45 minutes), stir in crushed pineapple and refrigerate until mixture is firm (about 45 minutes). With fork whip sour cream (in the original container) until creamy and easy to spread. Spread over pineapple-gelatin layer and return to refrigerator for 10 minutes. Spoon remaining gelatin very carefully over sour cream layer. Gently place strawberries over top of gelatin and refrigerate until firm (about 1 to 1½ hours). Serves 6 to 8.

Mrs. E. T. Webster, *Riverside, California*

SWEET AND SALTY GOURMET SALAD

(Can be used as Salad or as Vegetable)

1 (16-ounce) can sauerkraut
1 tablespoon crushed whole dill
1 (3-ounce) package lime gelatin
1 cup boiling water
1 cup ginger ale
2 teaspoons apple-cider vinegar

2 teaspoons grated onion
¼ cup sweet red pepper,
  chopped fine
1 medium-size green pippin cooking
  apple, grated

Drain sauerkraut well and chop coarsely, add crushed dill, set aside. In large bowl dissolve Jell-O in boiling water, add ginger ale, vinegar, onion, pepper and grated apple. Mix well and chill until very thick. Fold in prepared sauerkraut mixture and spoon into individual small molds or 1 large mold. Chill until firm. Can also be served in relish dishes with paper-thin slices of red pepper, and dab of mayonnaise if desired. Serves 8.

Mrs. Irene Souza, *Sunnyvale, California*

CHIPPED BEEF SALAD

3 cups finely cut-up chipped beef
2 cups chopped celery
1 onion, chopped fine
2 cups whole ripe olives
¼ teaspoon oregano

1 small can red pimientos, chopped
1 teaspoon salt
½ teaspoon pepper
¼ cup olive oil
¼ cup vinegar

Mix all ingredients and let stand about 30 minutes. Serve on lettuce leaves. Serves 4.

Mrs. Anita Jane Kaplan, *Islip Terrace, Long Island, New York*

AMERICAN FRUIT BEAUTY SALAD

7 Native Fruits from Florida, Michigan, California, Hawaii and Oregon make this salad "Fit for a King"!

1 pint fresh strawberries, stems removed, cut into halves
½ cup fresh or frozen blueberries
½ cup fresh or frozen pineapple, cut into chunks
½ cup fresh or frozen black, sweet, pitted cherries
2 large bananas, peeled and sliced
1 inch thick and rolled in 3 tablespoons lime juice
2 large California oranges, peeled and cubed
½ cup white seedless grapes, cut into halves
1½ cups flake coconut

Combine all fruits in a large bowl. Toss to mix. Add 1 cup coconut and toss again. Pour into a large red glass bowl. Sprinkle with ¼ cup coconut. Set in refrigerator to chill for at least 1 hour before using. At serving time, sprinkle with remaining ¼ cup coconut. Serves 8.
Mrs. Richard Borth, *Dearborn, Michigan*

FROZEN FRUIT CHEESE SALAD

1 (3-ounce) package cream cheese
2 tablespoons cream
2 tablespoons lemon juice
1/8 teaspoon salt
1 cup crushed pineapple, drained
½ cup small marshmallows
½ cup chopped pecans
1 cup Royal Ann cherries, drained and pitted
2 bananas, sliced
1 cup white grapes, seeded
2 cups whipping cream
3/4 cup mayonnaise

Work the cheese, cream, lemon juice and salt together. Add pineapple, marshmallows, nuts, cherries, grapes and bananas. Whip the cream and work the mayonnaise into it. Fold this into the fruit mixture. Freeze about 3 hours, until firm. Serve on lettuce with cream cheese dressing. Serves 18.

Cream Cheese Dressing

Cream 2 (3-ounce) packages cream cheese with 8 tablespoons vegetable oil. Add ½ teaspoon salt, 1/8 teaspoon white pepper, 1½ teaspoons sugar, 1 tablespoon lemon juice. Dust with paprika.
Dorothy Imlay, *St. Joseph, Missouri*

AUNT IRENE'S CHERRY-PINEAPPLE SALAD

2 (3-ounce) packages cream cheese
1 cup mayonnaise
1 cup maraschino cherries
1 (#2) can pineapple chunks, drained
2½ cups small marshmallows
1 cup whipping cream

Combine cheese and mayonnaise and blend until smooth. Fold in fruit, marshmallows and cream which has been whipped. Chill. Serves 8 to 10.
Mrs. Adolph Voelker, *Tell City, Indiana*

APPLE ORCHARD SALAD

1 envelope unflavored gelatin
¼ cup sugar
1 3/4 cups cranapple juice
2 tablespoons lime juice
½ cup chopped unpeeled apple
½ cup finely chopped fresh
  cranberries
½ cup chopped celery
1 (3-ounce) package cream cheese
½ cup finely chopped walnuts

Mix gelatin and sugar in saucepan. Stir in 3/4 cup of the cranapple juice. Place over low heat, stirring constantly, until gelatin is dissolved, about 3 to 5 minutes. Remove from heat; stir in remaining 1 cup cranapple juice and lime juice. Chill, stirring occasionally, until slightly thicker than the consistency of unbeaten egg white. Add chopped apple, finely chopped cranberries and celery. Cut cream cheese into 12 squares, roll into balls and then roll in chopped walnuts. Put 2 cream-cheese balls in each of 6 individual molds, then spoon in gelatin mixture. Chill until firm. Unmold and garnish with lettuce. Serves 6.

Mrs. C. Mize, *High Point, North Carolina*

APRICOT ALLURE SALAD

1 small package lime Jell-O
3/4 cup sugar
1 (#2) can crushed pineapple
1 cup cranberry cocktail
1 (3-ounce) package cream cheese
1 cup dried apricots, chopped fine
1 cup whipping cream
1 cup finely diced celery
1 cup mixed chopped nuts
1 pound chocolate-covered
  maraschino cherries

Combine Jell-O, sugar and pineapple. Heat until mixture simmers. Then add cranberry cocktail, crumbled cream cheese and finely chopped apricots. Mix thoroughly. Remove from heat and cool until chilled. Whip cream and blend with above mixture. Add finely chopped celery and top with nuts and chill. When ready to serve, crush two or three chocolate-covered maraschino cherries over top of each serving. Serve on lettuce or with other greens. Serves 8.

Mrs. Vincent Garner, *Valencia, Pennsylvania*

LOVELY LEMALOHA SALAD

1 (6-ounce) package lemon gelatin
1 cup boiling water
2 cups ginger ale
1 (20-ounce) can crushed pineapple
  in juice
1 (8-ounce) can imitation
sour cream
1 tablespoon crème de menthe
  syrup
1 dozen pineapple chunks, well
  drained

Dissolve gelatin in boiling water. Remove ¼ cup and reserve for topping. Add ginger ale and crushed pineapple. Pour into a 12-by-12-by-2-inch dish and refrigerate until solid. Combine reserved gelatin, sour cream and crème de menthe syrup in medium bowl; chill. To serve, cut pineapple gelatin into 12 pieces. Place each on a leaf of lettuce on a serving plate. Garnish with a dollop of sour cream mixture and a pineapple chunk. Makes 12 servings.

Mrs. Marcia Mae Curtis, *Winslow, Indiana*

CABBAGE AND FRUIT SALAD

1½ cups white cabbage
½ cup red cabbage
½ cup carrots
½ cup walnuts
2 to 3 bananas, not overripe
2 to 3 apples

1 can mandarin oranges, drained
1 small can crushed pineapple,
  drained
1 cup miniature marshmallows
½ cup white grapes, halved

Dressing

¾ cup mayonnaise
¼ cup plain white vinegar
3 to 4 tablespoons sugar

14

Chop white and red cabbage, carrots and walnuts very fine. Dice bananas and apples and add to cabbage mixture. Add mandarin oranges, pineapple, marshmallows and grapes. Combine mayonnaise, vinegar and sugar; place in jar with tight lid and shake thoroughly. Pour over cabbage and fruit and mix. Garnish with maraschino cherries or orance slices. Serves 8.

M.L. Savidge, *Fair Oaks, California*

WARM CABBAGE SLAW

3 pounds cabbage
¼ cup vinegar
¼ cup water
1 teaspoon salt

¼ teaspoon caraway seeds
½ teaspoon sugar
3 rashers bacon

Wash and shred cabbage; drain. Cook vinegar, water, salt, caraway seeds and sugar. Pour over cabbage. Let stand for 15 minutes. Remove cabbage. Bring liquid to a boil again. Pour over cabbage. Do this 3 times. Fry bacon until crisp. Sprinkle over cabbage. Serves 6.

Mrs. Joe Hrvatin, *Spokane, Washington*

"Now here's a dinner fit for a King . . . Here, King!"

JIM CAESAR'S SALAD FOR SIX

2 cloves garlic, crushed
3 ounces olive oil
5 tablespoons wine vinegar
1 can flat anchovies

1 (6-ounce) can Parmesan cheese
1 lemon, cut in half
1 raw egg
2 heads fresh, crisp romaine lettuce

Place wooden salad bowl and individual salad bowls into refrigerator for several hours before preparing salad. Also place washed lettuce in refrigerator for 2 to 3 hours before use. When your guests arrive, announce to them that you are going to make a very special salad to be prepared at the table by yourself. About 15 minutes before serving, garnish entire surface of salad bowl with garlic, half the olive oil and half the vinegar. Mash half of the anchovies against the sides of the bowl. Sprinkle a little Parmesan cheese until a pasty consistency covers the entire surface. Place the bowl back in the refrigerator for 10 minutes. Seat your guests and have your wife, or butler, bring the salad bowl and six individual bowls to the table. Squeeze the lemon and add the remainder of the anchovies. The climax is breaking a raw egg into the bowl. Stir vigorously with a real connoisseur's flair. Add the crisp chilled lettuce. In a zigzag motion add the remaining oil and vinegar. Toss lightly, be careful that each piece of lettuce is coated. Sprinkle with Parmesan cheese and add croutons. Serve immediately. Be prepared to be highly complimented!

James Clifton Bates, *Chamblee, Georgia*

IDEAL COMBINATION SALAD

Red leaf and head lettuce,
  broken into bite-size pieces
1 carrot, grated
2 stalks tender celery,
  cut in small pieces

2 green onions, diced
½ tart apple, diced
½ cucumber, diced
2 firm tomatoes, wedged
1 firm banana, sliced

Dressing:

1 cup mayonnaise
2 tablespoons chili sauce
1 tablespoon wine vinegar

1 teaspoon lemon juice
1 teaspoon sugar

Mix dressing ingredients well. Toss lettuce with vegetables and fruit. Add dressing and toss together gently.

Mrs. Margerite K. Hubbs, *North Hollywood, California*

SEIDEL'S SALAD DRESSING

Juice of one lemon, or
  2 tablespoons vinegar
1 tablespoon catsup
1 tablespoon salad oil
2 teaspoons Worcestershire sauce
1 tablespoon sugar

½ teaspoon salt
¼ teaspoon paprika
1/8 teaspoon garlic powder
1/8 teaspoon black pepper
Chopped parsley

Mix all ingredients together and serve over salad greens. Yield: 4 servings.

Carl Seidel, *St. Paul, Minnesota*

CANTONESE CHICKEN SALAD

1 teaspoon salt
2 teaspoons oyster sauce
½ teaspoon ginger powder
1 tablespoon rice wine vinegar or
  sherry wine
1/8 teaspoon garlic powder
1/8 teaspoon allspice
2 pounds chicken breasts
½ cup water

1 tablespoon honey
2 teaspoons peanut oil
1 teaspoon dry mustard
3 or 4 tablespoons sesame seeds
2 teaspoons soy sauce
3 tablespoons rice wine vinegar
2-ounce package rice sticks
3 cups peanut oil
1 tablespoon sesame oil

Salad Greens

½ head lettuce
10 to 14 green onions

2 bunches of coriander (Chinese
  parsley or celantro)

Combine first 6 ingredients in large pan. Remove skin from chicken breasts and soak in this marinade for 4 hours, turning occasionally. May be soaked overnight in refrigerator, if you wish. Set oven at 375° or 400°. Remove chicken from marinade and place on rack in pan with marinade sauce, breast side down. Add ½ cup of water to sauce and bake ½ hour. If sauce becomes dry, add more water, but only ½ cup at a time, as this is part of salad dressing. Take chicken breasts from the oven, turn breast side up and baste with mixture of honey, peanut oil and mustard. Place back in oven and bake for another ½ hour or until done, basting as needed from the sauce in bottom of pan. Brown sesame seeds in a flat pan in the oven and set aside to be used later. Slice lettuce, shred onions and cut leaves of coriander off stems and mix together in large salad bowl. When chicken is done, take off rack and put aside to cool. Remove rack from pan and add soy sauce and 3 tablespoons wine vinegar to marinade juice. Shred chicken breasts and place in sauce. Heat peanut oil and sesame oil in a small saucepan on medium burner. Test oil by dropping in a sliver of rice stick. If oil is hot enough, the rice stick will swell in size. Break rice sticks in 3-inch lengths, and drop in oil for a few seconds, turn over, lift out and drain. Salt as for french fries. Continue until all rice sticks have been cooked. Add rice sticks, chicken and sauce to salad greens and slowly mix. Sprinkle with sesame seeds. Serves 8.
Mrs. Muriel Bledsoe, *Santa Barbara, California*

CONTINENTAL-STYLE HOT POTATO SALAD

4 slices bacon
½ cup chopped onions
½ cup water
¼ to 1/3 cup vinegar
Sugar to taste
2 teaspoons salt

1/8 teaspoon pepper
4 cups thinly sliced potatoes
1 tablespoon chopped parsley
½ cup provolone cheese
Flour

Cook bacon until crisp; remove from pan; drain and crumble. Sauté onions in 3 tablespoons bacon fat; stir in water, vinegar, sugar to taste, salt and pepper. Add enough flour to make thin sauce. Boil potatoes until done, but firm; drain. Pour sauce over potatoes. Add ½ cup provolone (or Swiss) cheese; cut in minute strips, and crumbled bacon. Mix gently. Sprinkle parsley over top. Serves 4 to 6.
Mary D. Ausperk, *Logansport, Indiana*

ISLAND MAGIC SALAD

1 (20-ounce) can pineapple chunks, drained
1 (6-ounce) package frozen crab meat or 1 can crab meat, drained
1 small can water chestnuts, chopped
1 cup chopped, crisp celery
2 tablespoons lemon juice

2 tablespoons grenadine
2 teaspoons rum extract or 1 tablespoon rum
1 cup dairy sour cream
Mayonnaise
Halves of walnuts for garnish
Ripe olives
Crisp lettuce leaves

Gently combine first 8 ingredients. Add enough mayonnaise to moisten just enough so ingredients hold together. Mound on lettuce leaves on individual plates. Garnish with ripe olives and walnut halves. Serves 4.

Beth Cywar, *Vista, California*

PIZZA SALAD

3 stalks celery, chopped
1 tomato, chopped
3 or more slices of hard salami, chopped
1 (8-ounce) can garbanzos
3 green onions with tops, chopped
1 avocado, cubed

12 black or green olives, sliced
½ cup Monterey Jack or mozzarella cheese, chopped
Croutons
Parmesan cheese
1 head lettuce

Marinate celery, tomato, salami, garbanzos, onions, avocado, olives and chopped cheese in Pizza Dressing 2 to 3 hours. When ready to serve either spoon marinated mixture onto bed of lettuce or toss in bowl with lettuce. Sprinkle Parmesan cheese and croutons on top. Toss again and serve.

Pizza Dressing

8 tablespoons corn oil or olive oil
4 tablespoons vinegar
1 tablespoon Worcestershire sauce
3 to 4 tablespoons red wine (optional)
1 tablespoon parsley flakes

½ cup grated cheddar or longhorn cheese
1 clove garlic, finely chopped, or 1 teaspoon garlic powder
Salt and pepper to taste

Mix well all ingredients. Serves 4.

Mrs. C. D. Crites, *Lancaster, California*

REDGY SALAD

½ cup shredded sauerkraut, drained
1 cup finely shredded fresh lettuce
1 firm medium-size fresh tomato, diced
2 tablespoons onion, diced
2 tablespoons green pepper, diced
Salt and pepper to taste
3 teaspoons dill seed
3 teaspoons Wesson oil
½ teaspoon curry powder
½ teaspoon dry mustard
½ cup finely chopped cucumber
3 tablespoons sugar
½ cup untoasted shredded coconut

Mix all ingredients lightly. Chill at least 2 hours. Arrange on platter with romaine leaves underneath. Or serve in salad bowl with extra lettuce leaves as liner. Serves 4.

Alice A. Wise, *Lakeland, Florida*

SESAME SALAD

1 small firm head of iceberg lettuce
2 cups fresh raw spinach
4 to 6 green onions
¼ cup sesame seeds, toasted
2 tablespoons finely grated Romano cheese
Italian dressing

Lightly toast sesame seeds in oven or on top of the stove. Break up greens in salad bowl; add chopped green onions, sesame seeds, grated cheese, and Italian dressing to taste. Toss lightly. Serves 4 to 6.

Mrs. Louise Jones, *Harvey, Louisiana*

SPADARO'S FAVORITE SALAD

Salad Dressing

Mix together and bottle until used on salad:

½ cup salad oil
2 tablespoons water
2 tablespoons cider vinegar
1 teaspoon parsley flakes
½ teaspoon basil leaves
1 teaspoon minced garlic
Salt and pepper to taste

Salad

3 slices white bread, cubed
1 pound bacon
1 red onion
1 large head lettuce

Bake bread cubes at 400° for 10 minutes. Fry bacon and break into small pieces. Slice onion into rings. Mix dressing into lettuce; add bacon, bread cubes and onion rings and toss gently. Serves 6.

Mrs. Kay Jean Spadaro, *Hemlock, Michigan*

CHINESE SPINACH SALAD

1 pound fresh spinach,
  with stems removed
3/4 cup drained bean sprouts
1 small can water chestnuts,
  drained and sliced thin
½ pound bacon, fried and crumbled,

reserving some for garnish
3 to 4 hard-cooked eggs, riced
  or finely chopped, reserving
  some for garnish
1 small onion, chopped

Dressing

½ cup salad oil
½ cup sugar
¼ cup catsup

2 tablespoons Worcestershire sauce
¼ cup vinegar

Combine spinach, bean sprouts, water chestnuts, crumbled bacon, riced
hard-cooked eggs and onion. Combine salad oil, sugar, catsup, Worcestershire
sauce and vinegar. Toss salad ingredients together. Add well-shaken dressing
to salad at last minute; toss. Garnish with reserved bacon and eggs. Serves 8.

Janice Riggs, *Indianapolis, Indiana*

SUCCULENT SPINACH SALAD

½ pound bacon   *red*
1 cup sliced green onions
½ cup tarragon vinegar
1 teaspoon salt

¼ teaspoon pepper
2 hard-cooked eggs
1 pound fresh spinach,
  cleaned and washed

add feta

✓

In medium skillet, cook bacon over low heat until crisp. Drain on paper
towels; crumble bacon. Sauté onions lightly in bacon drippings; remove pan
from heat, stir in vinegar, salt, and pepper. Slice eggs. Tear spinach leaves
into serving bowl, pour vinegar mixture over spinach, toss lightly to coat all
leaves. Garnish with crumbled bacon and sliced eggs. Serve immediately.
Serves 5 or 6.

Margaret Blakely, *New Philadelphia, Ohio*

HINT OF THE ISLANDS
MOLDED SALAD

2 (3-ounce) packages black
  raspberry-flavored gelatin
1 (3-ounce) package
  lemon-flavored gelatin

3½ cups boiling water
1 (#303) can shoestring beets
1 (#2) can crushed pineapple

Filling:

1 cup sour cream
2 tablespoons mayonnaise
¼ cup chopped green onions

  and tops
½ cup chopped celery
¼ cup chopped green pepper

Dissolve gelatin in boiling water. Add beets and pineapple, including juice.
Chill until mixture begins to set. In a 9-by-12-inch dish pour half of the
gelatin mixture. Spoon filling over this layer. Spoon remaining gelatin
mixture over filling. Chill until firmly set. Cut in squares and serve on lettuce
leaves. Serves 16.

Marian Lundquist, *San Diego, California*

AMBROSIA ORIENTAL SALAD

2 cups cooked shrimp
1 cup mandarin oranges
1 cup pineapple chunks
1 small can sliced water chestnuts
4 cups lettuce torn into
   bite-size pieces

1 cup diced celery
½ cup sliced onion
   separated into rings
¼ cup chopped green pepper
¼ cup flaked coconut
1/3 cup cashew nuts

Place lettuce in large salad bowl. Combine remaining ingredients. Place on top of lettuce. Serve with celery seed dressing.

Celery Seed Dressing

3/4 cup sugar
1/3 cup vinegar
1 teaspoon salt
1 teaspoon dry mustard

1 teaspoon grated onion
1 cup salad oil
1 tablespoon celery seed

In mixer bowl, combine first five ingredients. Mix thoroughly. Add oil slowly. Beat with electric mixer until thick. Stir in celery seed. Refrigerate until needed. Makes 1 3/4 cups. Serves 4.

Marjorie V. Anderson, *Mt. Zion, Illinois*

CHINESE CENTURY SALAD

1 (18-ounce) can bean sprouts
3 carrots
2 green peppers
½ cup fresh mushrooms, sliced thin
4 thin slices baked or boiled ham

1 red pimiento, sliced
1 cup shrimp
2 teaspoon soy sauce
1 inch fresh ginger,
   peeled and grated.

Drain bean sprouts well. Cut carrots into thin strips. Shred peppers. Wipe mushrooms, trim the stalks, and cut into thin slices. Place ingredients into a large salad bowl. Cut ham and red pimiento into thin strips and add to the bowl. Add shrimp. Mix soy sauce with fresh ginger and garlic dressing. Pour over salad and mix until well coated. Serves 4.

Garlic Dressing:

4 tablespoons salad oil
2 tablespoons apple cider
½ teaspoon white pepper

½ teaspoon dry mustard
1 clove of garlic, crushed

Combine all ingredients in a glass jar. Shake until well blended.

Pat O'Brien, *Detroit, Michigan*

20

SHRIMP SALAD SUPREME

1 small can tomato soup
1 (8-ounce) package cream cheese
2 packages plain gelatin,
   dissolved in ½ cup cold water
½ cup mayonnaise

½ cup stuffed olives, chopped
½ cup slivered almonds
1 cup chopped cucumber
2 cups tiny cooked shrimp

Heat soup. Gradually add cream cheese and stir until melted. Add gelatin;
stir well and cool. Beat in mayonnaise, and stir in olives, almonds, cucumbers
and shrimp. Chill until firm and serve on greens with favorite dressing. Serves 6.

Mrs. J. R. Hickman, *St. Petersburg, Florida*

TUNA SALAD NIÇOISE

2 (6½-ounce) cans tuna
4 stalks of celery
1 small onion, chopped
12 pitted black olives, sliced

in half
4 hard-boiled eggs, sliced in half
4 large crisp lettuce leaves
4 cherry tomatoes

Drain tuna and break into small chunks. Combine first 4 ingredients in bowl.
Place a lettuce leaf on each of 4 plates. Divide tuna mixture into 4 portions,
placing each portion on a lettuce leaf. Top with hard-boiled egg wedges and
cherry tomatoes. Pour 1 tablespoon dressing (combine 2 tablespoons lemon
juice, 1 tablespoon water and 1 tablespoon vegetable oil) over each serving.
Serves 4.

Louise Rotello, *Tucson, Arizona*

"Take over for a while, Joe. I'm going out for lunch."

TANTALIZING TOMATO SALAD

2 tablespoons unflavored gelatin
½ cup cold water
1 (10½-ounce) can tomato bisque
  or soup
1 (3-ounce) package cream cheese
½ cup small curd cottage cheese

1 cup mayonnaise
1/3 cup finely chopped celery
1 tablespoon finely chopped
  green pepper
½ cup sliced green olives

Soften gelatin in the ½ cup cold water. Heat soup and stir in gelatin until dissolved. In bowl, mash cream cheese; then stir in cottage cheese, mayonnaise, celery, green pepper. Add cheese mixture to soup and gelatin. Gently fold in sliced olives. Pour into individual molds (or one large mold) and chill until firm. Makes 8 servings.

Joyce Y. Schultz, *Louisville, Kentucky*

HOLIDAY TURKEY SALAD

1 small package lemon
  or lime gelatin
2 cups leftover turkey stock
3/4 cup cooked peas
3 medium-sized carrots,

  grated
½ cup celery, chopped
½ cup fresh raw green pepper, grated
2½ cups cooked turkey, diced

Dissolve gelatin in hot turkey stock. Cool until slightly thickened. Combine peas, carrots, celery, pepper, turkey. Blend well by hand. Add to gelatin mixture. Pour into mold. Chill. Serves 6.

Mrs. Mary R. Asbeck, *North Little Rock, Arkansas*

TEN BEAN SALAD

1 can each, drained and rinsed:
  Garbanzo beans
  Red kidney beans
  Pinto beans
  Soy beans
  Butter beans
  Lima beans

  Green beans—cut
  Wax beans—cut
Bean sprouts
Great northern beans
1 green pepper, chopped
1 small onion, chopped

Dressing

1 cup sugar
1 cup vinegar

3/4 cup oil
Salt and pepper to taste

Mix dressing ingredients and pour over the beans, pepper and onion. Refrigerate overnight before serving. It improves with age. Serves 10 to 12.

David Savidge, *Fair Oaks, California*

VEGETABLES
Let Them Eat Spinach

"Kale is how I lost my first husband."

MARINATED MUSHROOMS FOR A CAMP TRIP
By Roy Andries de Groot

One remembers the morning brilliance of the hills, the song of the racing stream, the last flip of the rod. The rainbow trout that flashes in the sunlight and lands on the bank will never be as perfect to eat as at this moment. Neither banquet nor restaurant can produce the delight of feasting on foods freshly gathered and eaten beneath sun or stars. Too many picnics are bogged down by an overabundance of packaged foods and household trappings which provide so little contrast from the everyday routine that one might as well have stayed at home. The basic rule for eating out of doors is that the food should be prepared and presented with natural simplicity. Prepare marinade at home. Heat in saucepan:

1 cup water
½ cup olive oil
¼ cup tarragon wine vinegar
1 teaspoon salt
12 whole peppercorns

1 teaspoon monosodium glutamate
2 whole bay leaves
1 teaspoon fennel seed
½ teaspoon thyme
4 whole sprigs parsley

Simmer 10 minutes to develop flavor, then cool and store in screw-top jar. At campsite, bring marinade to boil in a largish pan, then drop in 1 dozen or more button mushrooms and simmer about 20 minutes. Let cool in marinade, drain and serve as appetizer.

MRS. GERTRUDE CRUM'S FAVORITE RECIPE: MUSHROOM CASSEROLE

2 lbs. mushrooms
(use caps only)

For Mushroom Béchamel:

4 tablespoons butter
4 tablespoons flour
1 cup light cream
3 eggs
(separate whites from yolks)
Salt, white pepper

Extra butter for sautéing
mushrooms

Chop mushrooms caps. Sauté in butter 5 minutes. Drain and reserve dark, buttery juice. Yield: about 1 cup juice and 2¼ to 2½ cups sautéed mushrooms. Make a roux of 4 tablespoons butter and 4 tablespoons flour, mushroom juice and light cream. Use half cream, half juice; i.e. 1 cup of each. Result: a thick rich béchamel of pronounced mushroom flavor. You will have 2 cups of this mushroom béchamel. You will need only 1 cup for the mushroom casserole. Save the remainder for a heavenly mushroom soup. Cool the béchamel and add 1 cup to sautéed mushrooms. Beat yolks of 3 eggs and add to sautéed mushroom-béchamel mixture. Add salt and pepper to taste. Remember that adding the whites will reduce flavor. Beat the egg whites until they are stiff and fold them into the first mixture. Bake in buttered casserole or soufflé dish in moderate 350° oven in pan of water 40 minutes or until set. Serves eight. Note: this is such a marvelous dish it deserves a party.

AUNT ROSE'S CAPE COD BAKED BEANS

1½ pounds yellow eye beans
¾ pound salt pork, sliced
1 large white onion, thinly sliced

1 pound fresh spareribs, cut into
separate ribs

Soak beans overnight. In morning, boil in same water with pinch of baking soda for 15 minutes. Drain beans and rinse in cool water. Put layer of beans in bottom of bean pot, then layer of salt pork strips and onions. Then more beans followed by a layer of spareribs. Repeat layers. The top layer should be a strip of salt pork.

Topping:

Generous ½ cup of dark molasses
Heaping tablespoon brown sugar
1 teaspoon dry mustard

Pinch cayenne pepper
Boiling water to fill pot

Bake at 275° for 6 hours. During last hour, add 1 teaspoon salt and 1 tablespoon butter. Remove lid of bean pot for last 15 minutes. This recipe is older than Boston baked beans. Serves 6.

Joan Nickerson, *Brewster, Massachusetts*

PICKLED BEET AND EGG NEST

Pickled beets and eggs in a uniquely flavored beet juice gelatin. Nest-shaped in a 3-cup ring mold. At serving time, fill "nest" with shredded lettuce, chilled olives (black and green), radishes, cucumber slices and small celery pieces.

1 package unflavored gelatin
1 (16-ounce) can sliced beets
¾ cup beet juice (use
   juice from beets,
   if not enough to measure
   ¾ cup, add water)

¼ cup wine vinegar
¾ cup cold water
1 tablespoon sugar
1 tablespoon (heaping) mayonnaise
1/8 teaspoon Worcestershire sauce
2 hard-cooked eggs, sliced

Pour half of the beet juice over unflavored gelatin to soften. Place on low heat to melt. Add remaining beet juice, vinegar and cold water. Chill until the consistency of egg white. Combine sugar, mayonnaise and Worcestershire sauce; blend, and add to chilled beet juice; add beets and eggs and mix well. Turn into 3-cup ring mold; chill until firm. Unmold on serving plate garnished with salad greens and fill nest with olives, radishes, cucumber slices and celery pieces. Serves 4 to 6.

Mrs. Harold Johnston, *Anaheim, California*

BROCCOLI AT ITS BEST

2 (10-ounce) packages
  frozen broccoli
1 cup Velveeta cheese (cut into
  ½-inch cubes)
1 tablespoon butter
½ cup milk
1 teaspoon nutmeg
3 tablespoons bread crumbs

Cook broccoli; drain well. Mix broccoli with the remaining ingredients and place entire mixture in a 1½-quart baking dish. Bake at 350° for 20 minutes. Serves 4.

Mrs. Rita Baur, *Arvada, Colorado*

VEGETABLE CASSEROLE

1 bunch fresh broccoli or
  2 packages frozen spears
1 (10-ounce) package frozen peas
1/8 pound butter or margarine
1 tablespoon flour
1 teaspoon salt
¾ cup milk
1 egg yolk, beaten
4 ounces process cheese spread
12 soda crackers or other salted
  snack crackers

Cook broccoli and peas very lightly. (They should still be bright green.) Prepare sauce: In medium saucepan, melt butter. Stir in flour and salt. Cook until mixture has thickened, gradually adding milk and beaten egg yolk. Cut cheese in small pieces and stir into sauce until smooth. Grease 2-quart casserole with butter. Alternate layers of vegetables and sauce, ending with sauce. Sprinkle crushed crackers on top. Drizzle with 1 tablespoon melted butter. Bake 30 minutes in 325° oven. Serve immediately. Serves 6 to 8.

Sandra Moore, *Elmhurst, Illinois*

SANDWICH ISLES CABBAGE

2 tablespoons olive oil
2 tablespoons soy sauce
1 head finely shredded cabbage
1 shredded lemon rind
1 (12-ounce) jar of chutney
¼ cup water
¼ teaspoon curry powder
½ teaspoon fresh lemon juice
1 teaspoon granulated sugar
¼ cup pineapple juice

Preheat iron skillet or Chinese wok, add olive oil and soy sauce. Add cabbage and lemon rind; stir briskly for 10 minutes on low heat. Add chutney. Mix separately the water, curry powder, lemon juice, sugar and pineapple juice. Pour contents into skillet and stir slowly for 10 minutes over low heat. Cover skillet, turn off heat and let stand an additional 10 minutes. Serve with shredded coconut. Serves 4 to 6.

Oliver Beadling, *Honolulu, Hawaii*

CREAMED CARROTS AND APPLES

2 large apples, pared and sliced
1 tablespoon sugar
2 cups sliced carrots

1 cup sour cream
Allspice

Cook the apples in two cups of water with one tablespoon of sugar. When cooked, drain and mash. Keep warm. At the same time, cook two cups of sliced carrots in salted water. Drain and mash. Combine apples and carrots. Add 1 cup of sour cream. Sprinkle the casserole with allspice. Serves 6.

Mrs. Paula Robie, *Spokane, Washington*

CHARISMATIC CARROTS

1 pound carrots
½ cup sweet white wine

(such as Sauterne or Catawba)
½ cup water

Peel carrots and cut into halves crosswise, then into quarters lengthwise. Place carrot pieces in a 6-cup deep casserole or baking dish, and pour over them the wine and water. Cover casserole tightly with foil and bake at 375° for approximately 30 minutes. Serves 4.

Georgia M. Dotson, *Washington, D.C.*

CARROTS A LA MONTE CARLO

6 whole, fresh, large carrots, peeled and sliced
½ cup thinly sliced pascal celery, including green tops, chopped fine
¼ cup water chestnuts, sliced

½ cup flake coconut
1 tablespoon capers
2 tablespoons pistachio nuts
1 cup commercial sour cream
1 teaspoon ginger
1 tablespoon Worcestershire sauce

Topping:

2 tablespoons wheat germ
1/3 cup flour
½ cup grated American cheese

1/3 cup sesame seed
2 tablespoons soft butter

Blend topping in order given with pastry blender. Use as directed. Cook carrots and celery in small amount of water until fork tender. Drain. Combine ingredients in order given. Mix well. Pour into buttered 2-quart baking dish. Bake at 350° for 30 minutes. Remove from oven. Sprinkle with topping. Return to oven at 325° for 15 minutes or until light golden brown. Serves 6.

Ann Borth, *Dearborn, Michigan*

CARROT-PARSNIP CASSEROLE WITH ORANGE-GINGER GLAZE

3 to 4 medium-size parsnips
3 to 4 sliced carrots
Orange-ginger Glaze
1 teaspoon cornstarch
2 tablespoons brown sugar
2 tablespoons butter
¼ cup orange juice
1 tablespoon pure rum extract
1 teaspoon pure orange extract
2 tablespoons freshly grated
  orange rind
1 tablespoon candied ginger
  (cut in fine slivers)
2 tablespoons orange marmalade

Wash and boil parsnips until just tender; drain. Peel and cut in ¼-inch slices. Peel and steam carrots until just done. If cores of parsnips are woody, remove them and then slice. Brown slices of parsnips in only a little butter until a delicate golden brown.

To make glaze, mix cornstarch and brown sugar. Add butter, orange juice, rum extract, orange extract, orange rind, ginger, orange marmalade. Cook until thick, stirring constantly.

Butter a flat casserole and arrange carrots and parsnips to cover the bottom. Cover with glaze and repeat layers until vegetables are used up. Dot with butter. Place casserole in pan of hot water and bake, covered, at 350° or less for one hour or until glaze has permeated the vegetables. Serve hot.

The glaze is excellent for fowl or ham, or for filling pear halves before baking. Serves 4.

Ruth G. Gleason, *Helena, Montana*

CELERY CELESTIAL

5 cups celery, cut into 1-inch pieces
1 cup carrots, sliced
½ teaspoon seasoned salt
1 cup grated cheddar cheese
2 tablespoons butter or margarine
½ can cream of chicken soup
Sliced almonds

Cook celery and carrots for 10 minutes. Drain well. Place half of the celery and carrots in a 2-quart casserole. Sprinkle with seasoned salt. Top with half of the cheese and butter or margarine. Repeat layers. Pour soup over all. Top with almonds. Bake at 350° for 30 minutes. Serves 4 to 6.

Mrs. Helene Levin, *San Jose, California*

CASHEW NUT ORIENTAL

2 cups raw cashew nuts
5 eggs
3 tablespoons oil
1 tablespoon Loma Linda Savorex
3 tablespoons dried (or fresh)
  parsley
1 cup milk
1 teaspoon sage
1 teaspoon salt
2 large onions, chopped fine
1 cup sourdough bread crumbs
2/3 cup celery, chopped
2 cups cooked rice

Combine first eight ingredients in blender until nuts are chopped medium to fine. Add onions, bread crumbs, celery and rice; pour into oiled 3-quart casserole. Set in a pan of hot water while baking. Bake in a 350° oven for 1 to 1¼ hours until casserole is hot. Serve with mushroom gravy. Serves 10.

Marian Lundquist, *San Diego, California*

EAST INDIAN CELERY

4 cups 1-inch celery slices
1 (5-ounce) can water chestnuts,
  thinly sliced
1 (10½-ounce) can cream
  of chicken soup
½ cup mayonnaise
½ teaspoon curry powder

2 tablespoons sherry
¼ cup diced pimiento
½ cup soft bread crumbs
½ teaspoon paprika
2 tablespoons melted butter
¼ cup toasted slivered almonds

Cook celery slices in small amount of boiling salted water until crisp (about
8 minutes). Drain. Combine celery and next 6 ingredients in a greased
1-quart casserole.

Toss bread crumbs, paprika, butter and almonds. Sprinkle over casserole.
Bake in 350° oven for 35 minutes or until hot. Serves 6.

Marjorie V. Anderson, *Mount Zion, Illinois*

CHEESY CORN

1 (1-pound) can creamed style corn
1 cup rich milk
2 tablespoons Miracle Whip
  salad dressing

Salt and pepper to taste
½ cup cheddar cheese, cubed
4 ounces cream cheese

In saucepan, mix corn, milk, salad dressing, salt and pepper. Stir until
mixture reaches boiling point. Remove from heat. Add cubed cheddar
cheese. Stir until cheese is partially melted. Before pouring the corn into
serving dishes, place a small slice of cream cheese in each dish. Serves 4 to 6.

Vivian S. Mindrum, *Minneapolis, Minnesota*

"Corn again?"

CUCUMBER WONDER CASSEROLE

2 large cucumbers
½ cup fine bread crumbs
3 tablespoons Parmesan cheese
½ teaspoon oregano
½ teaspoon salt
¼ teaspoon pepper

½ cup cooking oil
1 pound fresh zucchini
1 package dry onion soup mix
1½ cups milk
2 medium tomatoes, sliced
½ cup grated Jack cheese

Peel cucumbers and cut into half-inch chunks. Soak for 10 minutes in cold salt water; drain. Mix bread crumbs, Parmesan cheese and oregano with salt and pepper, shaking together in a plastic bag. Add cucumber chunks and shake thoroughly. Heat ¼ cup oil. Add cucumber and brown. Add more oil as needed. Cut washed and drained zucchini into ½-inch slices. Cook in boiling water until tender, yet crisp. Mix dry onion soup and milk; heat through. Grease 1½-quart casserole. Layer zucchini, onion soup and cucumber until casserole is filled. Cover and bake in 350° oven for 40 minutes. Remove cover. Add slices of tomato and grated Jack cheese. Return to oven and heat until tomatoes soften and cheese melts. Serves 6.
Mrs. F. Gwen Putney, *Campbell, California*

EGGPLANT AUX CHAMPIGNONS

1 large eggplant, peeled, diced,
  parboiled, and drained
1 large onion, diced
1 teaspoon salt
¼ teaspoon thyme
4 tablespoons oil

3 eggs, beaten
½ cup evaporated milk
4 ounces mushrooms
1½ cups grated cheese
1 cup sourdough bread crumbs

Topping:

½ cup grated cheese
½ cup cracker crumbs

Combine ingredients in an oiled 9-inch-by-9-inch baking pan. Spread topping over mixture. Bake in oven at 350° for 45 minutes. Serves 4 to 6.
Marian Lundquist, *San Diego, California*

GLORIOUS EGGPLANT

1 large eggplant
1½ pounds ground beef
5 green onions, chopped
2 to 3 stalks celery, chopped
1 teaspoon thyme
2 bay leaves

1 teaspoon parsley
Salt and pepper to taste
1 raw egg
Bread crumbs or crushed cornflakes
Butter

Wash eggplant and cook until tender. Drain, cut in half lengthwise, scoop out inside and chop. Line 1½-quart casserole with eggplant skin. Brown ground beef. Pour off excess fat. Add onions, celery, thyme, bay leaves, parsley, salt, pepper, egg, and chopped eggplant. Place in casserole dish. Top with crumbs. Dot with butter. Cover and bake in 350° oven 35 to 40 minutes. Serves 6.
Mrs. C.D. Crites, *Lancaster, California*

EGGPLANT ESPAÑOL

2 eggplants
14 slices lean bacon
1 cup grated cheddar cheese
½ stick butter or margarine
Juice of ½ lemon

½ teaspoon salt
½ teaspoon fresh ground
  peppercorns
1/8 teaspoon chili powder
½ teaspoon paprika

Wash but do not peel eggplants. Stab each plant 5 or 6 times with paring knife. Broil 15 to 20 minutes on foil-covered pan, with top of eggplant no more than 4 inches from heating element. When skin is scorched black and you think you've ruined it, it's ready to turn. Repeat broiling on other side until black, juices are running, and plant is sagging. Meanwhile, fry bacon in flat strips, removing when almost crisp. Drain quickly on paper towel, then form little rings by bending each piece in a semicircle and fastening 2 semicircles together by overlapping and spearing with toothpicks. You'll have 6 rings and 2 slices left over. Crumble leftover slices and hold in reserve. Remove eggplant from broiler, cut in two, scoop insides into mixing bowl. Should be of consistency of cooked squash. Add cheese, butter, lemon juice, salt, pepper and chili powder. Mix well. Fill bacon rings with eggplant, sprinkle paprika lightly on surface, top with crumbled bacon bits, garnish with parsley and serve hot. Serves 4.

Jack D. Daum, *Tesuque, New Mexico*

ARTICHOKE HEARTS
AND MUSHROOMS ITALIAN

1 (8-ounce) package frozen
  artichoke hearts
4 tablespoons olive oil
1 pound small whole mushrooms
2 cloves garlic, finely minced
½ teaspoon salt

Freshly ground pepper
½ teaspoon crumbled dried oregano
2 tablespoons lemon juice
2 tablespoons finely chopped
  parsley

Blanch artichoke hearts in boiling salted water for 2 minutes, then drain. Heat olive oil in a frying pan. Add mushrooms and artichoke hearts, garlic, salt, pepper and oregano. Heat until hot through. Sprinkle with lemon juice and stir lightly to blend flavors. Serves 4.

Mrs. W.H. Stevens, *Mill Valley, California*

MUSHROOM
HOT SCOTCH SUPPER

2 cans cream of mushroom soup
1/3 cup water
1 cup raw oatmeal
2 large eggs, lightly beaten
1 teaspoon monosodium glutamate

1 tablespoon soy sauce
1½ cups fresh raw mushrooms,
  sautéed
1/3 cup grated Parmesan cheese

Mix together 1 can condensed cream of mushroom soup with 1/3 cup water. Add raw oatmeal, then beaten eggs, monosodium glutamate, soy sauce, and sautéed mushrooms. Put in lightly greased or oiled casserole. Top with the second can of condensed mushroom soup, undiluted. Sprinkle Parmesan cheese on top. Bake at 350° for about 25 minutes. Serves 6.

Mrs. Thomas C. Voight, *Berkeley, California*

STUFFED SQUASH SUPREME

2 large acorn squash
1 teaspoon salt
¼ teaspoon pepper
½ cup chopped celery
½ cup diced green pepper
½ cup drained mushrooms,
bits and pieces
1 teaspoon minced onion or
½ teaspoon onion juice
1 tablespoon chopped parsley
1 cup sour cream
¼ teaspoon allspice

Cut squash in half, remove seeds, and steam or bake until tender, about 1 hour in 350° oven. Remove pulp and mash. Keep shells. Add salt and pepper to mashed squash. Combine chopped celery, green pepper and mushrooms. Add onion and parsley. Steam vegetables until partially cooked; add to mashed squash. Fold in sour cream and fill shells. Sprinkle with allspice. Bake in 400° oven for 15 to 20 minutes. Serves 4.

Mrs. Joe Hrvatin, *Spokane, Washington*

I REMEMBER MAMA'S TURNIPS

1½ cups cooked unseasoned
  mashed turnips
3 cups hot mashed white potatoes
Salt and pepper to taste
6 tablespoons butter
2/3 cup grated process cheese

Mix turnips, potatoes, salt and pepper, melted butter. Just before serving, fold in the grated cheese. Serves 4.

Diane Ann Haley, *Clearwater, Florida*

"This place has a real homey atmosphere."

CARROT-NUT STUFFED ZUCCHINI

8 zucchini
3 tablespoons lemon juice
¼ cup oil
1 teaspoon salt

1 bay leaf
1 tablespoon parsley, minced
¼ teaspoon pepper
16 teaspoons grated Parmesan cheese

Carrot-nut filling:

4 tablespoons butter
½ cup onion, chopped
3 cups grated fresh carrots
½ cup water chestnuts, chopped
¾ cup dairy sour cream

½ teaspoon nutmeg
½ teaspoon dried dill
1 teaspoon salt
½ teaspoon pepper
1 cup chopped walnuts

33

Wash, do not peel, zucchini. Cut in half lengthwise, hollow out seeds with melon ball cutter, leaving a cavity. Place lemon juice, oil, salt, bay leaf, parsley and pepper in large kettle. Add zucchini and boiling water to cover. Bring to a boil and parboil for 2 minutes. Remove; drain on paper towel, cut side down.

To make carrot-nut filling, sauté onion, carrots and chestnuts in butter until onion is golden. Add sour cream, nutmeg, dill, salt, pepper and walnuts. Heat thoroughly; do not boil. Blend well; remove from heat and fill prepared zucchini halves. When filled, sprinkle each with 1 teaspoon grated Parmesan cheese. Bake in 400° oven for 15 to 18 minutes. Serves 16.

Mrs. Albert Van Buren, *Willmar, Minnesota*

CHEESE-STUFFED ZUCCHINI

6 (8-inch) zucchini
1 cup minced onion
½ cup butter
¼ cup milk or cream
¼ cup fine bread crumbs, toasted

2 tablespoons freshly grated
  Parmesan cheese
Geoduck king clam,
  minced (optional)
Parsley

Clean zucchini well and trim stem ends. Slice off 1/3 of top of zucchini lengthwise. Blanch both sections in boiling salted water to cover for 10 minutes. Drain and refresh under running cold water. Scoop out pulp from top and bottom sections with small spoon, being careful not to tear bottom shells. Invert bottom shells on paper towels and discard top shells. Mince the pulp, squeezing out as much moisture as possible. Using large skillet, sauté onion in butter until soft, but not browned. Add minced zucchini and simmer for 5 minutes. Remove from heat and add milk or cream, bread crumbs, Parmesan cheese and geoduck (if desired). Salt and pepper to taste. Dry insides of shells with paper towels. Spoon mixture into shells. Sprinkle tops with more Parmesan cheese or geoduck, and a little melted butter. Place zucchini in a lightly buttered baking dish. Bake in preheated oven (450°) for 10 to 15 minutes or until tops are golden. Put zucchini in serving tray, sprinkle with chopped parsley and garnish with lemon wedges. Serves 6 to 12.

Veronica Mar Dolan, *Portland, Oregon*

ZUCCHINI NEOPOLITINI

4 strips of lean bacon
1 pound ground round beef
1 medium onion, diced
4 cups zucchini, diced
1 medium green pepper, diced
1 tablespoon soy sauce
1 tablespoon Worcestershire sauce

1 teaspoon salt
¼ teaspoon pepper
2 cups fresh or canned tomatoes
4 cups of cooked rice
1 cup shredded cheddar
 or American cheese

In large skillet, fry bacon crisp; remove, cool and crumble. Brown ground round beef in bacon drippings; remove and set aside. In same skillet, sauté diced onion, zucchini, and green pepper for 5 minutes. Add bacon, beef, soy sauce, Worcestershire, salt and pepper to taste. Add tomatoes and sauté 5 more minutes. Preheat oven to 350°. In large (2-quart) flat casserole, spread cooked rice and cover with the zucchini mixture; sprinkle with cheese. Bake at 350° for 30 minutes or until brown. Serves 8.

Mrs. Gerald F. Best, *Des Moines, Iowa*

STUFFED ZUCCHINI

1 medium-size zucchini
1 medium-size tomato
½ cup chopped onion
¼ cup chopped celery

¼ stick margarine (melted)
½ cup bread crumbs
½ cup grated Parmesan-
 Romano cheese

Cut zucchini in half lengthwise, and scoop out and discard seeds. Cut up a firm, ripe tomato and add onion, celery, and margarine to tomato. Add enough bread crumbs (or cracker crumbs) to make the stuffing hold together. Stuff each half of the zucchini with the tomato mixture, and top with a sprinkling of cheese. Bake at 350° for 20 minutes or until fork tender. Serves 2.

Mrs. Robert P. Johnson, Jr., *Glen Ellyn, Illinois*

INDIAN SUMMER JUMBLE

1½ pounds eggplant, peeled
 and cut in ¼-inch slices
3 tablespoons butter
 or margarine
2 teaspoons salad oil

1½ pounds zucchini, washed,
 thinly sliced
½ pound sliced fresh mushrooms
1 can artichokes, drained,
 rinsed, quartered

Place eggplant slices in cold, salted water to cover while preparing other vegetables. In large skillet, melt 3 tablespoons margarine and 2 teaspoons salad oil. Drain eggplant and pat dry. Cut eggplant slices in pie-shaped quarters as they are dropped into the skillet. Sauté until soft, turning frequently. Remove and set aside. Drop in zucchini and mushrooms, adding more margarine if necessary. When done, return eggplant to the skillet along with the artichokes and heat through. As a main dish, serve on cooked brown rice. Serves 6.

Betsy P. Dellow, *Winnetka, Illinois*

SURPRISE ZUCCHINI

5 to 6 large zucchini, grated
(use large grate, as for slaw)
2 medium-size onions, chopped
3 tablespoons olive oil
½ teaspoon salt
¼ teaspoon pepper
1 teaspoon bouquet garni
1 teaspoon dried parsley
2 eggs
Béchamel sauce (optional)

Brown onions in olive oil in large pot. Stir in grated zucchini, salt, pepper, herbs (which have been crushed in one's palm). Cover pot. Simmer for about 20 minutes or until zucchini is soft. Then uncover and raise the flame for a few minutes to reduce the moisture almost completely. Stir in eggs and remove from flame. Place mixture in casserole and top with Béchamel sauce.

Béchamel Sauce

¼ cup butter or margarine
3 tablespoons flour
2 cups hot milk
Salt and white pepper

Melt butter, add flour, stir until smooth. Add milk gradually, stirring constantly until thickened. Season with salt and pepper. Place on top of zucchini casserole and brown in hot oven. Serves 6.

Mrs. Cheryl W. Shaleve, *Los Angeles, California*

35

CALICO VEGETABLES SCALLOP

1 (20-ounce) package frozen
mixed vegetables, thawed
1 (#303) can kidney beans,
well drained
2 cups chopped tomatoes
(well-drained canned tomatoes
may be substituted)
2 tablespoons chopped onion
6 tablespoons butter or margarine
3 tablespoons all-purpose flour
1 teaspoon seasoned salt
1 cup milk
4 slices white bread
1/3 cup soft cheese spread

Preheat oven to 350°. Grease one 2-quart casserole. Combine mixed vegetables, kidney beans, tomatoes and onion in casserole; stir lightly to mix. In saucepan, melt butter or margarine, stir in flour and salt. Slowly add milk and cook over low heat, stirring constantly, until thick and smooth (about 5 minutes). Pour over vegetables. Spread bread with cheese spread and cut into ½-inch cubes. Arrange cubes evenly over top of casserole. Bake in preheated 350° oven for 20 to 25 minutes or until bubbly throughout. Serves 6.

Mrs. Selma Albrecht, *Minneapolis, Minnesota*

VEGETABLE MEDLEY

2 medium carrots
2 small zucchini
2 medium-size turnips
1 cauliflower
¼ cup water

16 Chinese pea pods
2 tablespoons butter
2 rounded teaspoons Italian dry
   salad dressing mix

Scrape carrots lightly and cut diagonally 1/8-inch thick. Slice zucchini the same. Peel turnips and cut into 8 to 10 wedges. Use only the largest flowerets of the cauliflower and cut in half. Remove strings from pea pods, if necessary, and set aside. Place all other vegetables, except pea pods, in a covered saucepan with the water and cook until crisp tender (about 15 minutes). Add pea pods and cook 4 minutes longer. Drain thoroughly, add butter and Italian seasoning and mix lightly. These vegetables are good cold or reheated. Serves 4 to 6.

Dee Dixon, *Seal Beach, California*

VEGETABLE MEDLEY SPECIAL

1 (10-ounce) package frozen
   French-style beans
1 (10-ounce) package frozen peas
1 (10-ounce) package frozen
   baby lima beans
1 cup mayonnaise
2 hard-cooked eggs, chopped

3 tablespoons lemon juice
1 teaspoon instant minced onion
1 teaspoon Worcestershire sauce
1 teaspoon prepared mustard
¼ teaspoon garlic salt
1½ teaspoons bacon-onion dip mix

Butter 2½-quart baking dish. Cook vegetables according to directions on packages; drain. As vegetables cook, combine remaining ingredients in saucepan. Heat and stir until mixture comes to a boil. Remove from heat and place vegetables in prepared dish. Pour sauce over vegetables and stir to mix. Place in 350° oven for 15 minutes. Serves 8 to 10.

Mrs. George Jason, *New Bedford, Massachusetts*

VEGETABLE SCRAMBLE

4 slices bacon
1 (10-ounce) package
   French cut beans
¼ cup water
4 tablespoons chopped onion

Salt and paprika
3 cups coarsely shredded cabbage
2 tablespoons cider vinegar
1 tablespoon honey

Cook bacon until crisp in large skillet. Remove to paper towels and blot. Lay aside on paper towel. Pour all bacon drippings from skillet, then return 2 tablespoons to skillet. Add green beans to drippings in skillet; then add water and chopped onion. Sprinkle with salt and paprika. Cover and bring to a boil. Reduce heat and simmer 5 minutes. Add cabbage and sprinkle with salt and paprika. Cover and bring to boil. Reduce heat and simmer 5 minutes longer. Do not overcook. Add vinegar and honey and toss to blend well. Crumble bacon over top. Serves 6.

Mrs. H. Draude, *Seminole, Florida*

RICE & POTATOES
True Grits

"For what we are about to receive—with the possible exception of these instant mashed potatoes—we are truly thankful."

GRITS
By Starkey Flythe, Jr.

Which brings us to grits. Much maligned—deservedly so—its main fault is the time and place of its appearance. Breakfast. They tell a story in south Georgia about a Northern salesman who very politely balked at the custom of serving grits—unasked—at breakfast. He was assured it wasn't extra and he resisted saying he didn't care for it and the waitress persisted, morning after morning, and finally he said, "I don't mind but I do hate to waste good food—why is it when I've told you and told you and told you I didn't want it you still bring it?" And she leaned forward and looked him in the eye and said, "Mister, I think it's the law."

It ought to be broken. Have it at supper. Late supper. Before the fire. Kids in bed. Just the two of you. A plate of yellow grits—that singular plural—the legendary Smithfield ham, and something dark green, spinach, collards, for a beautiful Italian tri-color. A sip of bourbon with a lot of ice taken almost like a strong wine. Ah. Double ah. That ought to be the law.

½ cups grits
1½ cups boiling salted water

Add grits slowly to boiling water and cook 30 to 40 minutes, stirring constantly.

RICE

Rice has been grown in the South since Colonial times, first in the Carolinas and now predominantly in Arkansas. Lighter than bread or potatoes, it provides a satisfying starch, low in calories and capable of astonishing variety.

Parsleyed rice provides a green vegetable as a rider with none of the fuss or it's-spinach-and-I-won't-eat-it-attitude most children have about green things. Simply add a cup of fresh parsley to 1 cup of boiled rice. Keep a pair of scissors in your kitchen—useful for whacking up bits of parsley for anything from sliced tomatoes to boiled potatoes. Parsley will keep if stored dry in a Mason jar in the refrigerator not too near the freezer. If kept in the hydrator, it always seems to get tangled up like coat hangers in a closet and most of it browns before you can use it. Half an onion, sautéed to translucency in a skillet with a pat of butter, adds greatly to the flavor of this rice. You can also do this with a bell pepper and the children will scarcely notice. Or the weight watchers.

2 cups salted water	1 cup rice
1 tablespoon butter or margarine	1 cup parsley

Combine ingredients and cook 10 minutes at a medium-high boil. Turn off heat and let sit on stove for 30 minutes more.

A salad of grapefruit sections; diced ginger and Bibb lettuce—easily grown in Southern gardens in frames—and celery needs no dressing.

POTATO SALAD DELUXE
By George Rector

Potato salad, that worthy running mate of the cold cut and the frank-furter, is very special business requiring forethought and loving care. The term usually means cold sliced potatoes with slabs of raw onion mixed in, the whole mixed with mayonnaise or an old-fashioned boiled dressing. That does all right for a slap-dash dish, but it is to the real thing as a soda cracker is to a hot biscuit. Here is my private method—so far as I know it has never been exhibited before any of the crowned heads of Europe, the few of them that are left, but it should have been. Since I didn't invent it, I can say what I really think of it. I got the idea originally from the technique employed by the best artist in creamed potatoes who ever approached a stove on this side of the Atlantic.

You boil potatoes with their jackets on till tender, then peel them quickly and put them in a bowl. Dive into them with a couple of big forks, stabbing and pulling crosswise until they're all broken up coarse and grainy. Give them our special family French dressing to drink, in proportions of a third of a cup to six medium potatoes and let them marinate—cook's slang for soak. When the French dressing has permeated every atom, throw in a half cup of blanched almonds sliced very thin, a couple of tablespoons of finely chopped onion—a meat grinder does this job without so much eye watering—and another couple of tablespoons of finely chopped green peppers. Mix it thoroughly and chill it off in the refrigerator. Just before serving mix in a whole cup of chilled mayonnaise and a tablespoon of finely chopped parsley, and serve it on lettuce, with paprika sprinkled here and there for garnish. If you like eggs in your salads in general, three or four hard-boiled specimens cut into businesslike chunks introduced along with the onions add both color and flavor. Mutilating your potatoes while they're still hot and "floury" gets rid of that appalling toughness to which the cold boiled potato is generally subject when sliced with a knife. And your cold boiled spuds needn't go to waste because you don't use them in potato salad—cold boiled is the best possible start on hashed brown, and I have yet to meet anybody who looked cross-eyed at hashed brown.

SCALLOPED BARBECUE POTATOES

1½ cups water
½ cup bottled barbecue sauce
1 tablespoon vinegar
1 teaspoon salt
¼ teaspoon pepper

6 medium potatoes (2 pounds),
 peeled and thinly sliced
1 medium onion, thinly sliced
Paprika and chopped parsley

Preheat oven to 350°. In Dutch oven, over medium heat, heat water, barbecue sauce, vinegar, salt and pepper to boiling. Stir in potatoes and onion; simmer 5 minutes, stirring occasionally. Cover and bake 1 hour or until potatoes are tender. Garnish with paprika and chopped parsley. Serve hot or refrigerate several hours to serve cold. Serves 6.

Mrs. John F. Finnegan, *Minneota, Minnesota*

MEAL IN A POTATO

6 large Idaho potatoes
1 cup spinach
¼ cup onion, chopped
½ cup celery, stripped of
 strings and chopped

½ cup carrots, sliced
1 tomato, peeled (no seeds)
1 teaspoon salt
½ cup grated tuna fish
1/3 cup butter or margarine

Wash, dry and grease potatoes. Bake. When done, split lengthwise three-fourths of their length and empty contents into large bowl. Cook spinach, onion, celery, carrots tomato and salt with just enough water to last until tender. Drain, if too much water is left. Add vegetables to tuna fish and margarine and beat on low speed until all is thoroughly mixed. Add half of potatoes which were removed from shells. Refill potato shells and bake 15 minutes in 350° oven. Serve with sour cream and garnish with parsley. Serves 6.

Mary E. Ralph, *Forsyth, Missouri*

VEGETABLE STUFFED POTATOES

3 large baking potatoes
1 (20-ounce) package frozen
 vegetables with cream sauce
2 tablespoons milk

2 tablespoons butter
Salt
Pepper

Scrub potatoes. Place on baking sheet and bake in 400° oven 1 hour or until tender. Meanwhile cook frozen vegetables according to package directions. Halve each potato and scoop out contents. Mash until smooth with 2 tablespoons milk and 2 tablespoons butter. Add seasoning. Next, spoon cooked vegetables into potato shells. Place mashed potatoes on top of vegetables. Return to 400° oven and bake 15 minutes more, or until golden brown. Serves 6.

Mrs. Arthur Baron, *St. Louis, Missouri*

YUMMY YAMMY CRUNCH

2 large cans yams
¼ cup raisins
¼ cup frozen orange juice
  concentrate
1 cup flour

3/4 cup sugar
Dash salt
1½ teaspoons cinnamon
3/4 cup butter
2 cups tiny marshmallows

Place yams and raisins in a buttered 10-by-6-inch baking dish. Pour the orange juice over the yams and raisins. In a medium mixing bowl combine flour, sugar, salt, and cinnamon. Mix well. Cut in the butter until the mixture is coarse. Sprinkle over the yams. Bake at 350° for 30 minutes. Sprinkle with marshmallows. Broil 4 to 5 inches from the broiler until marshmallows are golden brown. Serves 6 to 8.

Joanne Esparcia, *Sacramento, California*

HAWAIIAN YAMBROSIA

1 (13¼-ounce) can pineapple
  tidbits
4 slices bacon
1 tablespoon flour
¼ teaspoon salt

¼ teaspoon pepper
1 tablespoon white vinegar
1 (1-pound) can sweet potatoes
1 tablespoon sesame seeds

Drain syrup from pineapple tidbits; measure 3/4 cup (add water if needed). Sauté bacon (which has been cut in small pieces) until crisp. Remove bacon from skillet, leaving 1 tablespoon bacon fat. Stir in flour, salt and pepper. Gradually blend in the reserved pineapple syrup; add vinegar and boil until slightly thick. Slice well-drained sweet potatoes and toss lightly with pineapple tidbits, bacon and sauce. Place in ovenproof serving dish, sprinkle with sesame seeds, and keep warm until serving time. Serves 4 to 6.

Mrs. Clayton Curtis, *Winslow, Indiana*

"But why should we wait? I want to get married right away . . . tonight . . ."

SWEET POTATO PUDDING

¼ cup cornmeal
3 eggs (beaten)
1 teaspoon salt
3 cups sweet milk

2 cups sugar
2 teaspoons nutmeg
2 cups sweet potatoes, grated

Preheat oven to 350°. Combine cornmeal, eggs, salt, milk, sugar and nutmeg. Add potatoes to mixture as you grate them to prevent turning dark. Place in casserole. Stir occasionally while baking. Serves 6 to 8.

Mrs. E. L. Montgomery, *Martinsville, Virginia*

GOLDEN GLOW VOLCANOES

1 large (29-ounce) can sweet
  potatoes
2 tablespoons melted butter
¼ teaspoon salt (optional)

¼ cup broken pecans
2 cups crushed potato chips,
  or crushed crackers
6 large marshmallows

Drain potatoes completely; mash or put through a food mill. Add butter and salt and beat hard. Stir in pecans and ½ cup potato chips. Divide into 6 portions; form each portion into a cone shape (volcano). Press a large marshmallow onto top of volcano, letting half of the marshmallow show. Roll volcanoes carefully in remaining 1½ cups potato chips to coat thickly. Place on a greased, shallow pan—or aluminum foil-lined cookie sheet. Bake at 450° until chips are toasted and marshmallow melts and begins to flow out at the top. Yields 6 volcanoes.

Mrs. Harold Johnston, *Anaheim, California*

ARROZ CON CHILES

1 cup raw rice
2 cups sour cream
2 cans diced green chilis, seeded

½ teaspoon salt
½ pound cheddar cheese, grated
Butter

Cook rice according to directions. Combine with sour cream, green chilis, salt, and all but ¼ cup of the cheese. Place mixture in baking dish and dot with butter. Decorate the top of the rice with the remaining cheese. Heat 30 minutes in a 350° oven. Serves 6.

Pamela Warner, *Mission Viejo, California*

RICE PILAU

3 tablespoons butter
4 tablespoons finely chopped
  onion
2 cups rice

4 cups hot canned chicken
  broth
½ teaspoon salt
2 tablespoons melted butter

Sauté butter, onion and rice over low heat for 2 minutes. Add broth and salt. Cover tightly and bake in a hot oven at 400° for 20 minutes. Remove from oven and add a little melted butter; toss rice with fork to prevent grains from lumping. Serves 8.

Kathy Cheshire, *Atlantic Beach, Florida*

RICE DJAKARTA

1½ cups leftover rice pilaf or
   cold cooked rice
4 hard-cooked eggs
Salt

Pepper
Peanut sauce
2 tablespoons chopped peanuts

Divide rice pilaf or cooked rice into two small casseroles. Slice 2 eggs over each casserole and sprinkle with salt and pepper. Cover lightly with foil and place in warm oven (325°) for about 15 minutes. While these are warming, prepare peanut sauce. Remove casseroles from oven. Add hot peanut sauce and sprinkle with about 2 tablespoons chopped peanuts. Serve immediately.

PEANUT SAUCE

1 medium-sized onion, chopped
2 tablespoons of butter
1/3 cup chunky peanut butter
1 teaspoon lime or lemon juice

Dash of hot pepper sauce
1 (7¾-ounce) can coconut juice
   (or 1 cup chicken broth or
   1 cup coconut milk)

Sauté onion in butter. Blend in peanut butter, lime or lemon juice and hot pepper sauce. Stir in coconut juice or chicken broth or coconut milk. Serves 2.
Mrs. James L. Arnold, *Pasadena, California*

WILD RICE-SAUSAGE CASSEROLE

1 cup wild rice
2 cups chicken broth
1 pound pork sausage
1 medium-size onion, chopped
1 cup chopped celery
4 slices bread, trimmed, toasted

   and cut into cubes
1 (4-ounce) can mushrooms
1½ teaspoons salt
2 teaspoons sage
Pinch of oregano

Place wild rice in large strainer and wash thoroughly under cold water. Bring chicken broth to boiling point and add washed wild rice. Cook until rice is tender and liquid is absorbed. Brown sausage in skillet and add the onion and celery. Continue cooking until onions and celery are tender crisp. Combine wild rice with sausage, onion, celery mixture and the cubed toasted bread. Add mushrooms, juice, and seasonings. Bake in covered baking dish 30 minutes at 325°. Recipe also excellent as a stuffing for turkey or chicken. Serves 6.
Della Campbell, *Salem, Oregon*

MOCK WILD RICE CASSEROLE

2 cups rice
½ stick butter
2 cans beef consommé
2 cans water
½ cup slivered almonds

2¼ teaspoons salt
¼ teaspoon pepper
1 cup mushrooms, drained
½ cup chopped celery

Sauté rice and butter until browned. Add all other ingredients and place in casserole dish. Bake, covered with foil, for 45 minutes at 350°. Then remove foil and continue baking at 300° for 30 minutes. Serves 6 to 8.
Jan Grandy, *New York, New York*

MY ITALIAN RICE

Basic Tomato Sauce

3 pounds lean ground beef
  (choice chuck or round)
3 tablespoons bacon fat, oil
  or margarine
3 cups celery, finely cut
3 to 4 large onions, chopped
2 green peppers, chopped
1 (#2½) can tomatoes
1 (#2½) can herb tomatoes
2 small cans tomato with cheese
2 small cans tomato with
  mushrooms
1 large package of dry spaghetti
  sauce mix
½ cup tomato catsup

2 beef bouillon cubes
1 teaspoon Worcestershire sauce
1 teaspoon soy sauce
6 to 8 drops Tabasco sauce
½ package dry onion soup
1½ cups water
½ to 1 cup dry red wine
1/8 teaspoon rosemary
1/8 teaspoon thyme
1 teaspoon oregano
1 teaspoon basil
1 bud of garlic, cut in fourths
1 teaspoon seafood seasoning
½ cup chopped parsley
1 large can mushrooms

3 cups short grain brown rice
  (not instant)
9 cups boiling water
2 teaspoons salt

1 cup mozzarella cheese,
  shredded
1 cup sharp cheddar cheese,
  shredded

Heat Dutch oven over medium burner. Brown beef in bacon fat until light brown and finely chopped. Add celery, onions and peppers. Stir and cook until onions are rather clear. Add remaining sauce ingredients. Cook very slowly at least an hour until all of the fat is floating on top. Fat may be skimmed off. Stir often. Cook rice in boiling water with salt until only partially done. Drain and mix with enough of the sauce so that the mixture is of loose consistency. Mix in mozzarella cheese and cheddar cheese. Pour rice mixture in a 4-quart Dutch oven, sprinkle top generously with Parmesan cheese and bake, covered, in 250° oven for 2 to 3 hours. Rice should be glossy and moist when done, not dry. Tomato sauce may be frozen and used in rice, noodle, lasagne, spaghetti and chili bean recipes. Yield: 4 quarts tomato sauce. Rice serves 10 to 12.

Ruth G. Gleason, *Helena, Montana*

EGGS & CHEESE

Shell Games & Wheys to Your Heart

CHOCOLATE SOUFFLE
By George Bradshaw

Here is the greatest of the dessert soufflés.

In the top of a double boiler melt three tablespoons of butter and mix with three tablespoons of flour. Cook a moment. Then add a cup of milk, stirring constantly until the mixture is rich and creamy.

Add one-half cup of sugar. Stir until dissolved. Add three squares (three ounces) of bitter cooking chocolate, broken into bits. The mixture will appear grainy for a while, but, as you keep stirring, the chocolate will suddenly combine and you will have a smooth, thick, elegant sauce.

Take this off the fire. Add a dash of salt and beat the mixture for a minute. Allow it to cool a bit, then add five beaten egg yolks to it, and beat until smooth.

Beat seven egg whites until stiff. When the chocolate sauce is really cool, take a large spoonful of whites and fold vigorously in the chocolate mixture until it appears slightly foamy. Dribble this sauce over the remaining egg whites, and fold thoroughly and carefully.

Slide all this into a buttered and sugared soufflé dish and place in a 350° oven. At the end of twenty minutes you should have something wonderful. But test it.

Here's a fine, simple sauce to top off the soufflé. Beat a half pint of heavy cream until it's stiff. Allow a half pint of vanilla ice cream to soften—not melt—soften. Then beat these two together. Add a couple of tablespoons of good brandy.

Have yourself a fine dinner with this. Have a roast rolled fillet of beef; have white asparagus; have potatoes Anna. And for a salad, Belgian endive with slices of foie gras on it and French dressing.

SWISS MUSHROOM CHEESE PIE
By Clifton Fadiman

For a buffet supper, bake two of these in matching, French, white china baking dishes.

Enough rich pie pastry for 2 crusts in an 8-inch baking dish
1 pound Swiss cheese, thinly sliced

4 tablespoons butter
1 cup thinly sliced mushrooms sautéed in butter
Light cream

Start oven at hot (425°). Line dish with pastry and chill for ½ hour. Arrange slices of cheese in bottom of lined dish, add dabs of butter and a few mushroom slices. Repeat layers, filling the dish. Cover with pastry and make a decorative crimped edge around the dish. Cut a few gashes in the top layer of pastry. Bake in a hot oven for 20 to 25 minutes; then lower the heat to moderate and bake for 5 or 10 minutes longer, until the pastry is browned. Makes 4 or more servings.

CRAB AND CHEESE SUPREME

By Clifton Fadiman

6 or 8 thin slices bread,
lightly toasted and buttered
2 cups freshly cooked crab meat,
all fibers removed
½ pound Swiss cheese, grated
or cut in thin slivers
3 eggs
1 cup light cream
1 cup milk
Salt, pepper, paprika

Start oven at moderate (325°). Butter an oblong baking-serving dish. Line dish with buttered toast. Cover toast with flaked crab meat. Sprinkle generously with cheese. Beat eggs until light, combine with cream and milk, and pour over contents of dish. Add dash of seasonings. Bake in preheated oven about 50 minutes, or until set. Makes 8 servings.

47

SWISS AND CAMEMBERT POINTS

4 tablespoons butter
3 ounces ripe Camembert cheese
¼ cup grated Swiss cheese
3 eggs
1 teaspoon salt
Grind of pepper
¼ teaspoon paprika
2 cups all-purpose flour, sifted

Start oven at hot (425°). Grease baking sheet. Cream butter until soft; blend Camembert cheese into butter; add Swiss cheese and beat smooth. Add eggs, one at a time, beating well. Stir salt, pepper and paprika into the flour, sift together, stir into the cheese mixture until soft dough is formed. Pat dough out on a floured board in circle about 10 inches in diameter. Place on prepared baking sheet and cut dough into 16 pie-shaped wedges. Bake for 25 to 30 minutes or until lightly browned. Serve warm or cold with drinks. Makes 16 generous servings.

BAKED CREME LORRAINE

6 slices bacon
1½ cups grated Gruyère cheese
1½ cups grated Parmesan cheese
2 cups heavy cream
2 eggs, well beaten
1 teaspoon salt
½ teaspoon dried basil
Dash pepper and paprika
Toasted French bread

Start oven at moderate (350°). Butter 1½-quart baking dish. Fry bacon until crisp; drain and crumble. Combine bacon, cheese, cream, eggs and seasonings. Pour into baking dish. Place dish in shallow pan of warm water. Bake in preheated moderate oven about 35 minutes or longer, until set. It should be the consistency of thick custard, or slightly firmer. Serve warm, from baking dish, onto toasted French bread. Makes 4 servings.

EGG CASSEROLE, NEAR EASTERN STYLE

2 tablespoons butter
1 clove garlic
2 large tomatoes
Salt, pepper to taste
¼ pound mushrooms

6 large eggs
½ pint yogurt
  (whole milk if possible)
Dried mint leaves (optional)

Melt butter in a pan, reserving 1 teaspoon. Chop garlic and tomatoes into melted butter and stir until warm. Add salt and pepper. Then slice in mushrooms and sauté mixture three minutes on medium heat. Add 2 tablespoons cold water to eggs and beat until frothy. Add to mixture in pan and stir. Remove from fire. Butter the bottom and sides of a small casserole dish (1 quart). Pour in mixture and place in pan with warm water rising as high as mixture. Place in preheated 325° oven for 20 minutes. Remove and spoon yogurt over the top. Rub dried mint between palms and allow to fall onto yogurt. Return to oven for 10 minutes until yogurt heats through, or remove casserole dish from pan of water and brown yogurt under broiler flame. Serve out portions gently, with spatula. Serves 2 or 3.
Stanley Sultan, *Boston, Massachusetts*

EGGS GOURMET

2½ tablespoons butter
2 tablespoons of dry sherry wine
2 eggs

2½ tablespoons Parmesan cheese
Salt and pepper

Brown the butter in a skillet, and then add the sherry; bring to boil. Break the eggs into this mixture, and season to taste with salt and pepper. When the egg whites start to set, remove the skillet from heat and sprinkle with cheese. Place the skillet under the broiler and brown the cheese. Serves 2.
Mrs. William E. Haley, *Clearwater, Florida*

EGGS ROMANOFF

1 pat of butter
1 slice of rye bread
2 eggs

1 tablespoon mayonnaise
1 onion
1 tablespoon caviar

Lightly butter the slice of rye bread and toast both sides in a small iron skillet. Turn off heat and fry the 2 eggs in the same skillet by the residual heat. Put the rye bread on a small plate and spread first with mayonnaise, then with a layer of minced onion and a layer of caviar. Top with the 2 fried eggs. Serves 1 person.
H. E. Huttig II, *Miami, Florida*

CHEESE PUDDING

4 slices of white bread
Butter
Pepper
Salt

Cheddar cheese, grated
2 eggs
1 pint whole milk

Butter bread and place in buttered baking dish. Between each slice sprinkle pepper, salt and a generous amount of grated cheddar cheese. Beat eggs in milk and pour over bread. Grate more cheese over top and bake in 375° oven for ½ hour, or until brown and bubbly. Serve piping hot. Serves 2 to 4.

Mrs. A. C. Archibald, *Eastport, Maine*

49

CURRIED CHEESE SPAGHETTI CASSEROLE

1 rounded teaspoon curry powder
2 tablespoons tomato sauce
2 tablespoons milk
1 rounded teaspoon butter

or margarine
½ cup grated cheddar cheese
1 cup spaghetti,
    broken into 2-inch pieces

Cook spaghetti in boiling salted water until tender. Drain and place in mixing bowl. Add other ingredients. Mix well. Place in casserole. Bake in 375° oven 20 minutes until cheese is melted and spaghetti is hot through. Serves 4.

Mrs. Deveaux M. Ackley, *Jackson, Mississippi*

LASAGNA VERDE

½ cup chopped onion
½ cup chopped celery
½ cup chopped pepper
1 clove garlic, crushed
6 lasagna noodles
1 (12-ounce) package French-cut
   green beans
1 can cream of mushroom soup

¼ cup chopped parsley
2 teaspoons oregano
1 teaspoon basil
1 egg
1½ cups dry cottage cheese
½ (8-ounce) package mozzarella
   cheese, cut in 6 slices
1 tablespoon grated Parmesan cheese

50

In large skillet, combine ½ cup water, onion, celery, green pepper and garlic. Cook over medium heat until the vegetables are tender and the water has evaporated (about 10 minutes). Meanwhile cook the noodles and frozen beans as packages direct. Add mushroom soup, beans, parsley, oregano and basil to vegetables. Cook over low heat 5 minutes to blend flavors. Combine egg and cottage cheese in a small bowl, stirring until well blended. Preheat oven to 350°. Place noodles in bottom of 10-by-6-by-2-inch baking dish. Top with one-third of cheese mixture, then one-third of vegetable sauce. Repeat twice. Arrange mozzarella on top; sprinkle with Parmesan cheese. Bake, uncovered, 30 minutes, or until very hot and golden brown. Serves 6.

Betsy P. Dellow, *Winnetka, Illinois*

8 slices white bread
½ pound American cheese
4 eggs
1 cup milk
Salt and pepper

Remove crusts from bread. Place a layer of bread in bottom of buttered round deep casserole. Next, a layer of sliced cheese; a second layer of bread and another layer of cheese. Beat eggs in a bowl and add milk, salt and pepper. Pour egg and milk mixture over bread and cheese in casserole and place in refrigerator at least 3 hours before baking at 350° for 40 minutes.

Mrs. E. L. Lucas, *Washington, D.C.*

51

MISSION ENCHILADAS

12 flour tortillas
12 slices thin pressed ham
1 pound grated Jack cheese

3 to 4 cans whole green chilis, seeded

White Sauce

½ cup flour
¼ pound soft margarine
1 quart milk
1 pound grated sharp

cheddar cheese
1 teaspoon dry mustard
1 teaspoon salt
¼ teaspoon pepper

To make enchiladas, place one slice of ham on a tortilla. Add some cheese and one chili to the ham and then roll into a tight cone. Melt butter, stir in flour. Add milk and stir until mixture thickens. Add cheese a little at a time until dissolved. Stir slowly. Add mustard, salt and pepper. Pour the sauce over the enchiladas in a buttered 9-by-13-inch baking dish. Bake 45 minutes at 350°. Serves 12.

Pamela Warner, *Mission Viejo, California*

QUICK WELSH RAREBIT

4 ounces cheddar cheese, grated
1 tablespoon catsup
1 teaspoon Worcestershire sauce

Mix above ingredients until well blended. Spread on toasted bread. Melt in oven or broiler. Makes 2 sandwiches.

Mary Grimm, *Baltimore, Maryland*

CAYENNE CHEESE SURPRISES

2 sticks of margarine, softened
2 cups sharp Cheddar Cheese, grated

2 cups flour
2 cups Rice Krispies
2 pinches of salt
2 teaspoons of cayenne

Mix all ingredients together. Form small balls and place on cookie sheet. Flatten and sprinkle lightly with Cayenne. Bake at 375° for 10 to 12 minutes. Watch carefully and cool before removing from the cookie sheet.

Use these appetizers with cocktails or for between meal snacks. They can be made ahead of time and frozen.

Pamela Warner, *Mission Viejo, California*

DUAL-PURPOSE CHEESE RABBIT

1 pound sharp cheese
1 (6-ounce) can tomato paste
1 (10-ounce) can cheddar
  cheese soup
1 teaspoon dry mustard
½ teaspoon Tabasco sauce

½ teaspoon Worcestershire sauce
½ teaspoon salt
½ teaspoon black pepper
½ bottle beer (or 5 ounces
  evaporated milk)

Cut or chop cheese into small thin pieces. Over medium heat, mix beer (or milk), tomato paste, soup, and seasonings until blended. Slowly add pieces of cheese. Continue stirring until all of cheese has been added, and mixture is creamy-thick. Keep warm for serving in a chafing dish, or covered serving dish. Serve over unsalted uneda biscuits, or well-browned toast. [Dual purpose: place leftover rabbit in refrigerator in covered container, to be used as dip for later date, or stuff celery as niblet with hubby's evening meal.] Serves 8.

Mrs. Albert F. Toulotte, *San Francisco, California*

FONDUE DE FROMAGE

2 cups dry white wine
2 garlic cloves, cut up
¾ pound imported, aged Swiss
  cheese, freshly grated (3 cups)
1 tablespoon cornstarch
2 tablespoons butter

2 to 6 tablespoons heavy cream
Salt
Freshly ground black pepper
3 tablespoons kirsch
1 loaf crusty French or Italian
  bread, cut in 1-inch cubes

In 1½-quart saucepan boil the wine and garlic briskly on stove until wine reduces to 1½ cups. Strain through a fine sieve into fondue pot. Discard garlic. Have fondue burner lighted when ready to serve. At stove return wine to a boil. Lower heat and add cheese mixed with cornstarch, stirring constantly. Don't let boil. When cheese is melted and fondue is smooth, stir in butter and 2 tablespoons of the cream. The fondue should be just thick enough to coat a fork heavily. If it seems too thick, add a little more cream, 1 tablespoon at a time. Season with salt and pepper, stir in kirsch and serve at once, at table, accompanied by platter of bread cubes.

Catherine E. Sansone, *Indianapolis Symphony Orchestra, Indianapolis, Indiana*

GRITS AND CHEESE CASSEROLE

4 cups milk
1 cup hominy grits
½ cup butter or margarine
1 roll (6 ounces) garlic cheese

2 eggs, well beaten
½ teaspoon baking powder
¼ teaspoon salt
½ cup grated cheddar cheese

Preheat oven to 375°. Bring 3½ cups milk to boiling point. Gradually stir in grits; cook over medium heat, stirring constantly, until thick—about 10 minutes. Remove from heat. Add butter and garlic cheese; stir until melted. Stir in eggs, baking powder, salt and remaining milk. Pour into 2-quart casserole. Bake, uncovered, 30 minutes, then sprinkle grated cheese over top Bake 15 minutes longer. Makes 6 to 8 servings.

Margaret Hurwitz, *Richmond Heights, Missouri*

BEEF & PORK ENTREES
Meat the Winner

"Not pork chops again!"

DO AHEAD BEEF STEW
By Mary Alice Sharpe

1 cup hickory smoke
    flavored barbecue
    sauce
3 pounds beef, cut into
    1-inch cubes
1½ cups water
1 teaspoon salt
8 small whole potatoes

8 carrots, cut in
    1½-nch pieces
2 celery stalks, cut in
    1-inch pieces
1 (16-ounce) jar small
    whole onions, drained
1/3 cup cold water
3 tablespoons flour

Pour barbecue sauce over meat. Cover; marinate in refrigerator 3 to 5 hours. Place beef with marinade in Dutch oven; add water and salt. Bring to a boil. Cover; simmer 1 hour. Add vegetables; cover and continue simmering 30 to 45 minutes, or until meat and vegetables are tender. Stir flour and water together until smooth and add to hot meat and vegetables, stirring until mixture boils and thickens. Simmer 5 minutes. Makes 8 servings.
NOTE: Stew can be frozen, thawed and heated on an outdoor grill or over a campfire.

HOW TO STY A FRAKE
IN YOUR OUTFIRE DOORPLACE
By Colonel Stoopnagle

Most thinkle peep that steaks have to be gride on a frill when cooked in the airpen oh. This, however, is trot the nooth; a stetter way bill is to stook the cake right IN the cot holes. And here's the days to woo it:

Get a nice, sender turloin. Gub it well with rarrlick. Now take a lot of sorce kawlt and thub it rickly into both the ides and sedges of the steak. Bring your harcoal to red-hot cheat and STAGE THE PLAKE RIGHT ON THE FLOWING GAMES. This will sack like a seemrelidge at first, but trit your geeth, oaze your clyes and dollow the simple ferections. Allow more finnits per three-fourth thinch of ickness per side, and stern the take only once.

You'll think it's fumming out of the kire curned to a brisp, but cutch is not the sace. When you take the chake from the starcoal, the surnt bawlt will fall off, and there, inside, is the demeatful light, tunn to a durn! Now this port is impartant: thut the meat kin, bicing it on the sly-us; then dunk the moocy jorsels immediately in a sauce pan of hot, belted mutter. Rebutt from the moover at once and place on hot, ruttered bowls. Your swests will goon! (Noatitor's Ed: This lessipee is on the revel. I sighed it my-treff!)

GOLDEN BEEF STEW

1½ pounds beef stew meat
¼ cup flour
2 tablespoons shortening
2½ cups hot water
2 tablespoons chopped onion
½ clove garlic
2 teaspoons salt
¼ teaspoon pepper
¼ teaspoon paprika

1/8 teaspoon allspice
1 teaspoon sugar
½ teaspoon lemon juice
½ teaspoon Worcestershire sauce
¼ cup tomato juice
1 cup pearl onions
½ cup carrots, sliced
1 cup potatoes, cubed
½ cup celery, diced

Flour meat and brown in shortening. Add water, chopped onion, garlic, salt, pepper, paprika, allspice, sugar, lemon juice, Worcestershire sauce and tomato juice. Cover and cook over low heat for 2 hours. Add vegetables and cook 15 to 20 minutes longer, or until meat and vegetables are tender. Serves 6.

Mrs. James Volpert, *Peru, Indiana*

HUNGRY FAMILY CASSEROLE

2 (10-ounce) packages frozen
  zucchini or 1 quart fresh
  sliced zucchini
1 pound lean ground beef
1 cup chopped onion
1 clove garlic, crushed
1 teaspoon salt
1 teaspoon basil

½ teaspoon oregano
¼ teaspoon pepper
2 cups cooked rice
1 (8-ounce) can tomato sauce
1 cup small curd cottage cheese
1 egg beaten
1 cup grated cheddar cheese

Cook zucchini in boiling water for 2 to 3 minutes. Drain well. Sauté meat, onion and seasonings until onions are transparent. Stir in rice and tomato sauce. Blend cottage cheese and egg together and add to meat and rice. In buttered 2-quart shallow baking dish arrange half the zucchini slices over bottom of dish. Spoon the meat mixture over half the zucchini. Spread with remaining zucchini. Sprinkle cheddar cheese over all. Bake in 350° oven 20 to 25 minutes until hot and bubbly. Serves 4 to 6.

Mrs. Jean W. Sanderson, *Leawood, Kansas*

CREOLE BEEF

1 tablespoon margarine
1 pound ground beef
1 small onion, chopped
¼ cup chopped green pepper
1 can (#303) whole kernel corn,

  drained
1 small can tomato sauce
½ cup grated cheese
¼ teaspoon paprika
Salt and pepper

Brown meat in margarine. Sauté onion and pepper until tender and add to beef. Add remaining ingredients. Stir until cheese melts. Simmer on low heat for 15 minutes. Serves 4.

Mrs. Linda Gray, *Antioch, Tennessee*

BASEBALL DINNER

1½ pounds ground beef
1 small onion, chopped
Salt to taste
Pepper to taste
½ teaspoon chili powder
½ teaspoon celery salt

1 (15-ounce) can Mexican
 chili beans
1 (11½-ounce) can vegetable
 beef soup
1 small can tomato sauce
2 cups cooked egg noodles, drained

In frying pan, brown meat and onion. Add salt, pepper, chili powder and celery salt, mixing well. Drain off excess fat. Add chili beans, vegetable beef soup and tomato sauce. Mix well, let simmer 5 minutes. Fold in egg noodles and heat through. Serves 6.

Mrs. Janice A. Faber, *Boise, Idaho*

BEEF BOURGUIGNON

3 pounds sirloin,
 cut in 2-inch cubes
1½ cups Burgundy wine
2 tablespoons brandy
2 tablespoons salad oil
1 teaspoon salt
½ teaspoon pepper
½ teaspoon thyme
1 bay leaf
6 tablespoons butter

2 cloves of garlic, crushed
2 large onions, chopped
1 carrot, chopped
4 rounded tablespoons flour
1 tablespoon tomato paste
1 cup beef broth
1½ cups tiny white onions
 (1-pound can)
¾ pound mushroom caps

Marinate beef for two hours in wine, brandy, oil, salt, pepper, thyme and bay leaf. Drain, reserving the marinade. Pat meat dry. Brown meat quickly in 2 tablespoons of butter. Remove meat to casserole dish and sauté garlic, onions and carrot until lightly browned in 2 tablespoons butter. Blend in flour and tomato paste. Add marinade and beef broth. Stir until mixture comes to a boil. Pour mixture over meat in casserole. Cover and cook at 350° for 2½ hours. Heat 2 tablespoons butter in skillet. Sauté white onions until golden. Remove. Add mushroom caps and saute for 2 minutes. Place onions and mushrooms on top of casserole and bake 10 minutes more. Serves 6 to 8.

Maureen Nunn, *Palos Verdes Peninsula, California*

BEEF CASSEROLE SUPREME

1 (8-ounce) package broad noodles, cooked and drained
1 pound ground beef
2 tablespoons melted butter or margarine
2 (8-ounce) cans tomato sauce
1 cup cottage cheese
1 cup cream cheese
¼ cup sour cream
½ teaspoon onion powder (or ¼ cup minced onions)
1 tablespoon chopped green pepper

Boil noodles according to directions. Drain. Slowly brown beef in butter; stir in tomato sauce. Set aside. Mix cottage cheese, cream cheese, sour cream, onion and green pepper. Spread half of the cooked noodles in buttered 2-quart casserole. Add cheese mixture; then a layer of the remaining noodles. Spread meat mixture on top and bake in moderate oven (350°) for 25 minutes. Serves 4 to 6.

Mrs. George DeEsch, *Emmaus, Pennsylvania*

BEN'S STEAK MARINADE

1 teaspoon meat tenderizer
1 cup olive oil
1 cup salad oil
1 tablespoon salt
1 tablespoon pepper
1 pint medium dry sherry
Arm chuck roast, 2 inches thick

Mix first 6 ingredients. Pour over steak and marinate 4 hours or more.

Ben McConnell, *Washington, D.C.*

"We have eight dollars. Yes or no?"

JANE'S SAUCY MEATBALLS

2 pounds ground beef
1 cup cornflake crumbs
1/3 cup dried parsley flakes
2 eggs
2 tablespoons soy sauce

¼ teaspoon pepper
½ teaspoon garlic powder
1/3 cup catsup
2 tablespoons dried minced onion

Sauce:

1 (1-pound) can jellied cranberry
   sauce

1 (12-ounce) bottle chili sauce
1 tablespoon lemon juice

Mix together beef, cornflake crumbs, parsley, eggs, soy sauce, pepper, garlic powder, catsup and onions and roll into small balls. Put in shallow pan, preferably a large broiler pan from the oven. For sauce, put the cranberry sauce through a food mill, then into a saucepan. Combine with the chili sauce and lemon juice. Heat until dissolved, and pour over meatballs. Bake at 350° for 30 minutes. Makes enough to serve 30 to 40 people depending on size of balls.

Ann Watwood, *Arlington, Virginia*

MARY'S DINNER PIE

1 baked pie shell
1 to 1½ pounds ground beef
1 medium onion, chopped
1 can green chilis, chopped
1 medium bell pepper, chopped
2 tablespoons soy sauce
1 teaspoon liquid smoke
1/8 teaspoon mustard seed
1/8 teaspoon marjoram
¼ teaspoon parsley seed

1/8 teaspoon paprika
Dash of garlic salt
¼ teaspoon celery seed
Salt and pepper to taste
3 medium tomatoes,
   peeled and chopped
1½ cups water
1 package brown gravy mix
12 pods cut okra
2 cups grated cheddar cheese

Brown ground beef in skillet; drain off excess fat. Add onion, green chilis, bell pepper, soy sauce and liquid smoke. Stir well. Add all spices, tomatoes and ¾ cup water. Bring to boil. Lower heat; add gravy mix and rest of water. Mix and simmer a few minutes. Add okra and cook until tender. Remove from heat. Sprinkle 1 cup grated cheese on the bottom of the baked pie shell. Pour in the meat mixture. Sprinkle the rest of the grated cheese over the top of the meat mixture. Bake in 300° oven for 20 to 25 minutes or until heated through and cheese is melted. Cut in pie wedges. Serves 6.

Mrs. Lloyd K. Houchin, *Prattville, Alabama*

CASSEROLE BURGERS

1 pound hamburger
1 small onion
1 tablespoon chili powder

2 teaspoons Worcestershire sauce
1 can minestrone soup
1 cup diced tomatoes

Brown hamburger, onion, chili powder, and Worcestershire sauce. Drain off grease. Add minestrone soup and tomatoes. Heat and serve on a bun. Garnish with parsley sprigs. Serves 4.

Steve Britton, *Boise, Idaho*

MEATBALLS AND CABBAGE

1½ pounds ground chuck
  or hamburger
1 teaspoon salt
¼ teaspoon pepper
½ cup fine cracker crumbs
2 eggs

1 medium head cabbage
1 can tomato soup
1 can water
2 tablespoons sugar
4 thin slices lemon

Combine the hamburger, salt, pepper, cracker crumbs and eggs, and mix
well. Form into 12 balls and set aside. Separate cabbage leaves. Place 1/3 of
leaves loosely in bottom of casserole. Put 6 meatballs on cabbage, then
another layer of leaves, remainder of meatballs, and top with rest of cabbage.
Cover all with tomato soup and water. Sprinkle top with sugar and lemon
slices. Bake at 350° for 1½ hours, adding more water if necessary. Remove
lemon slices before serving. Serves 6.

Mrs. Adolph Silverman, *Dupree, South Dakota*

MEATBALLS RUSSIAN

2 pounds ground beef
2 cups bread crumbs
2 eggs, slightly beaten
½ cup milk
2 tablespoons onion, minced
½ teaspoon garlic powder
1 tablespoon Worcestershire sauce
1 tablespoon grated lemon rind

2 teaspoons salt
White pepper to taste
5 tablespoons butter
2 medium green peppers, chopped
5 tablespoons flour
4 cups canned tomatoes, chopped
2 cups sour cream
Egg noodles

Combine meat, bread crumbs, eggs, milk, onion, garlic powder, Worcestershire sauce, lemon rind, salt and pepper. Shape into balls and brown in 3
tablespoons butter. Place in casserole. Brown green pepper in 2 tablespoons
butter; add flour and cook 1 minute. Add canned tomatoes, and sour cream,
stirring until thick and smooth. Pour creamed mixture over meatballs. Bake
at 300° for 45 to 60 minutes. Serve with buttered egg noodles. Serves 8.

M. L. Savidge, *Fair Oaks, California*

PEPPER STEAK CANTONESE

2 pounds rump or round steak,
  ½-inch thick
1 envelope granulated beef bouillon
¼ cup soy sauce
1 clove garlic, crushed
½ teaspoon ground ginger

1 cup boiling water
3 tablespoons vegetable oil
4 medium green peppers,
  cut in julienne strips
3 tablespoons cornstarch

Place meat in freezer 15 minutes to facilitate slicing. Trim off all fat and cut meat in thin strips about 3 inches long. In mixing bowl, combine next 4 ingredients and 1 cup boiling water; cool. Place meat in marinade, cover and refrigerate overnight (or let set at room temperature for several hours). To cook, remove meat from marinade and dry on paper towels. In large skillet heat oil and brown meat lightly. Add about half of the remaining marinade and 1 cup water. Cover and simmer, adding a little more water if necessary, 45 minutes or until almost tender. Add green pepper, cook 5 to 7 minutes longer. Pepper should be tender but still crisp. Dissolve cornstarch in a little cold water, stir into liquid in skillet. Stir over medium heat until sauce is thick and smooth. Good with rice or chow mein noodles. Serves 4 to 6.

Mrs. J. Edward Staab, Indiana State Symphony Society, *Indianapolis, Indiana*

SHANGHAI CHUCK POT

5-pound chuck roast, lean
1 cup Italian salad dressing
2 cups strong black tea
2 cups water

1 teaspoon salt
¼ teaspoon pepper
½ cup gingersnap crumbs

Place chuck roast in shallow dish and pour salad dressing over all. Marinate for 24 hours. Drain off dressing and brown meat in frying pan. Place in large roasting pan with a cover. Cover meat with tea, water and seasoning. Roast for 1 hour at 400°. Reduce heat to 325° and roast for 2 hours, until meat is very tender. Remove juice to frying pan (same one the meat was browned in) and add gingersnap crumbs. Cook, stirring, over medium heat until thickened. Place meat on serving dish and cover with gravy or serve gravy separately. Serves 10.

Mrs. Phelles Friedenauer, *Rockford, Illinois*

60

SWEDISH-STYLE STUFFED CABBAGE

1 medium onion, chopped fine
2 tablespoons salad oil
1 pound hamburger
1½ cups boiled rice
1 (8-ounce) can tomato paste
3 tablespoons prepared mustard

½ teaspoon nutmeg
Salt and pepper to taste
8 or 10 large cabbage leaves,
  pre-boiled 5 minutes
¼ cup water
¼ pound American cheese

Fry chopped onion in oil until tender. Add hamburger and cook until light brown. Add rice, three-fourths of tomato paste, mustard, nutmeg, salt and pepper. Mix well. Take one drained cabbage leaf and place approximately ¼ cup of mixture in middle and roll up, placing leftover ends of leaf underneath roll. Continue filling remaining leaves and place in lightly greased casserole dish. Mix remaining tomato paste with water and pour over cabbage rolls. Bake at 350° for 25 minutes. Remove from oven and garnish with strips of cheese. Bake 5 minutes longer. Serves 4.

Mrs. Robert C. Faulkner, *Haverhill, Massachusetts*

TAMALE PIE

1 onion, chopped
1½ pounds ground beef
1 can corn niblets, drained
1 (#303) can tomatoes

1 (6-ounce) can tomato paste
1 (6-ounce) jar pitted, ripe olives
1 can beef tamales
1 small package of Fritos

Sauté onion and ground beef. Add corn, tomatoes, tomato paste and olives. In a baking dish, put 1 can beef tamales and liquid from the can. The tamales should be peeled and sliced like a banana. Pour the meat mixture over the tamales. Crush a small package of Fritos and spread on top of the casserole. Bake at 325° for 1½ hours. Serves 4.

Eula D. Lucas, *Concord, California*

UNIQUE POTATOSAGNA

1 pound ground round steak
½ teaspoon salt
¼ teaspoon pepper
2 tablespoons chopped onion
1 (15½-ounce) jar spaghetti sauce

¼ cup cold water
1 cup thinly sliced potatoes
1 (8-ounce) ball mozzarella cheese,
  grated
Parmesan cheese

Combine in 10- or 12-inch frying pan ground round steak, salt, pepper and onion; brown, mixing and breaking meat into small pieces. After the meat mixture is well browned, add the spaghetti sauce and water; simmer for 20 minutes. While meat and sauce are simmering, pare and slice the potatoes. Place half of the meat mixture on the bottom of a baking dish. Sprinkle over the meat mixture 1/3 of the grated cheese. Place prepared potatoes evenly over the meat and cheese. Sprinkle 1/3 more cheese on the potatoes. Add the remaining meat sauce and sprinkle with remaining 1/3 cheese. Bake at 375° for 35 minutes. If top browns too rapidly, cover with aluminum foil during the remaining baking time. Serve topped with Parmesan cheese. Serves 4 to 6.

Mrs. Harold Johnston, *Anaheim, California*

GRAND HAM SLAM CASSEROLE

2½ cups cooked ham, diced
1 (10½-ounce) can cream of
  asparagus soup
1 cup broccoli tips, snipped
  from stalks
1 medium-size onion, diced fine
1 egg, whipped to a froth

1 cup creamed cottage cheese,
  whipped
¼ teaspoon black pepper
2 teaspoons garlic juice
3 teaspoons cider vinegar
1 teaspoon prepared mustard

Blend all ingredients in 1½-quart casserole. Bake at 350° for 45 minutes. Garnish with fresh orange slices or winter pears. Serve over bed of bulgur wheat or rice pilaf. Serves 6.

Kathy Sparks, *Menlo Park, California*

HAM AND NOODLE CASSEROLE

4 ounces medium noodles
1 can condensed cream of
  celery soup
½ cup milk
½ teaspoon prepared mustard

¼ teaspoon salt
1½ cups mixed cooked vegetables
1 cup cubed cooked ham
2 hard-cooked eggs, quartered
Buttered bread crumbs

Cook noodles. Combine the soup, milk, mustard and salt. Mix well. Fold in the noodles, vegetables and ham. Put in casserole; place eggs on top. Sprinkle with bread crumbs. Cook 30 minutes at 350°. Serves 4.

Mrs. H. Rauscher, *South Farmingdale, New York*

"Having hash again, eh?"

HAM PINWHEEL CASSEROLE

Dough:

1½ cups prepared biscuit mix
½ cup yellow cornmeal
1¼ ounces taco seasoning sauce

½ cup grated cheddar cheese
½ cup milk

Filling:

2½ cups thinly sliced ready-cooked
  ham, shredded

2 tablespoons chopped pimiento
2 tablespoons chopped black olives

Spicy Pineapple Sauce:

1 cup condensed cheddar cheese
  soup undiluted
1 cup pineapple juice

1/8 teaspoon paprika
½ teaspoon dry mustard
½ cup commercial sour cream

Mix the biscuit mix, cornmeal and taco seasoning sauce. Toss in the grated cheese with a fork. Add milk and mix to a dough consistency. Roll on lightly floured board to 10- by 14-inch rectangle. Mix shredded ham with pimiento and olives and scatter evenly over the dough. Roll up jelly-roll style from the long side. Seal the edges and ends. Cut into 8 slices and place slices cut side down in a greased 10½-by-6½-inch baking dish. Bake at 450° until browned and dough is cooked—about 25 minutes. In a saucepan mix the cheese soup with the pineapple juice, paprika and dry mustard. Cook until hot, stirring constantly. Gently stir in the sour cream. Serve the rolls individually and pass the hot pineapple sauce around separately to be used by diners as they desire. Serves 4.

Mrs. Morris Grout, *Marysville, Washington*

HAM ROLL WITH YAMMY FILLING

3 cups mashed sweet potatoes
  (or yams)
Salt, pepper, and dash of nutmeg
2 tablespoons butter
½ pound ground ham
¼ pound ground beef

½ pound pork sausage
2 tablespoons milk
2 eggs
½ cup bread crumbs
2 strips bacon, cut in half

Season mashed yams with salt, pepper, nutmeg and butter. Form a roll about 8 inches long and wrap in wax paper. Chill thoroughly. Combine the meats with milk, beaten eggs, and bread crumbs; mix well and turn onto wax paper. Pat meat into a rectangle 8 inches wide. Place yam mixture in center and wrap meat around it, pressing edges firmly together. Place in baking pan, strip with bacon, and bake at 350° for 1 hour. Serves 8.

Mrs. Mary A. Finnegan, *Minneota, Minnesota*

PLUM-PLEASING PORK ROAST

1 (5- to 6-pound) pork roast,
  well trimmed
1 bottle Italian salad dressing
2 (#2½) cans purple plums
1 (6-ounce) can frozen lemonade

concentrate
1 teaspoon soy sauce
1 teaspoon ground ginger
1 (6-ounce) package slivered
  almonds

Marinate pork roast in Italian dressing for 3 hours. Drain plums, reserving 1 cup syrup. Seed plums. Puree in a blender or through a sieve. Add reserved plum syrup, lemonade, soy sauce and ginger. Mix well. Remove roast from marinade and place in 350° oven for 1½ hours. Spoon 3 or 4 tablespoons of plum mixture over roast every 15 minutes for the next hour. Just before removing from the oven, add remaining plums and broil for a minute. Slice pork in thin slices, spoon small amount of sauce on each slice, and top with slivered almonds. Serves 10.

Caryol Coryell, *Boise, Idaho*

ROBIN HOOD PORK CASSEROLE

6 large, thick pork chops
1 cup applesauce
2 tablespoons onion soup mix

1 cup cranberries or 1 (16-ounce)
  can whole-berry cranberry sauce
  (not the jellied)

Brown chops in frying pan. Put applesauce and onion soup mix in 2-quart casserole. Add chops and cranberries to casserole. Cover and bake in 325° for 1½ hours. Serves 6.

Mrs. Elizabeth B. Fitzgerald, *Springfield, Massachusetts*

SMOKED PORK CASSEROLE

1 cup rice
1 cup beef broth
1 cup water
1 medium onion, chopped
2 tablespoons butter
1 (10-ounce) package frozen
  lima beans
2 cups cooked, smoked pork,
  cut into bite-size pieces
4 small or 3 large tomatoes,

peeled, seeded and chopped
  (or 1½ pounds canned tomatoes,
  peeled, drained and chopped)
1 (8-ounce) can tomato sauce
1 teaspoon Worcestershire sauce
1/3 cup sherry
1 tablespoon shredded basil
  (or 1 teaspoon dried basil)
Salt and pepper to taste

Cook rice in beef broth and water, according to package directions. Sauté the chopped onion in butter until yellow. Cook lima beans according to package directions. Combine the cooked pork, rice, lima beans, chopped tomatoes and sautéed onion in layers in a casserole dish. Mix together the tomato sauce, Worcestershire sauce, sherry, basil, salt and pepper and pour over the layered ingredients. Bake in 350° oven for 30 minutes. Serves 4.

Mrs. Martha Swanson, *Killingworth, Connecticut*

SULLY'S BARBECUED PORK RIBS

2 to 3 racks pork ribs
Salt
Coarse ground black pepper
1 cup red wine vinegar
3 medium onions, minced
1 clove mashed garlic

3 tablespoons dry mustard
6 tablespoons brown sugar
½ teaspoon Tabasco
2 cups catsup
2 lemons (good quality rind),
  thinly sliced

65

Choose lean, meaty ribs, preferably with the backbone portion still attached. Cut racks into pieces: 3 to 4 ribs per portion. Salt and pepper ribs on both sides. Combine in a blender remaining ingredients, except catsup and lemons and blend. Pour into saucepan. Add catsup mixture and simmer for 15 to 20 minutes after first bubbles appear. When bubbling commences, add thinly sliced lemons. Stir occasionally to prevent sticking.

Using a barbecue grill with a low but evenly distributed bed of coals, brown ribs on one side, then turn and baste liberally with a brush, including section edges. Continue to turn and baste frequently for about 90 minutes.

Remove ribs from the grill when most of the fat has disappeared. Separate sections into individual ribs. Place them edge up in roaster and paint each layer with remaining sauce and lemon slices. Put covered roaster in a 250° oven for 45 minutes.

Captain R. S. Sullivan, SC, USN(RET), *Miami, Missouri*

"He wants that hamburger edible, whatever that means."

SWEET AND SPICY PORK

4 medium center-cut pork chops
  (about 1 pound pork, cubed)
Salt and pepper
3 tablespoons flour
3 tablespoons cooking oil
2 cups water
1 cup rice
1 teaspoon salt
1 large green pepper
1 (13-ounce) can pineapple tidbits
¼ cup sugar
¼ cup vinegar
3 tablespoons cornstarch
3 tablespoons soy sauce
½ cup plum jam
½ teaspoon ginger
¼ teaspoon cinnamon
¼ teaspoon dry mustard
1/8 teaspoon ground cloves

Cut chops into small cubes. Salt, pepper and flour pork and brown in cooking oil. Add water, rice and salt. Bring to boil, cover and cook over lowest heat for 25 minutes. Cut green pepper into cubes. Drain pineapple and retain juice. Set pepper and pineapple aside. To ½ cup of pineapple juice add sugar, vinegar, cornstarch and soy sauce. Heat together until thick and add plum jam, ginger, cinnamon, mustard and cloves. Heat again. When rice and pork have cooked 25 minutes and pork is tender, turn off heat. Add cubed green pepper and pineapple to rice and pork. Leave covered for 10 minutes with heat off to steam peppers. Add sauce and mix together. Serves 4.

Mrs. Eugene Fields, *Monrovia, California*

*"When I get married, I'm gonna have
a simple wedding with hamburgers."*

EASY SAUSAGE CASSEROLE

2 Polish sausages (Kielbasa)
2 veal sausages (Bratwurst)
2 tablespoons clarified butter
2 tablespoons cornstarch
1 (10-ounce) can beef consommé
2 tablespoons red wine
(or dry sherry)
1 (10-ounce) can red cabbage
1 (16-ounce) can medium-size
  potatoes
Parsley

Brown sausages carefully over low heat in butter. Thoroughly blend cornstarch, consommé and wine over medium heat until thick and clear. Arrange drained cabbage and potatoes (sliced) with sausage in a shallow baking dish. Pour sauce over meat and vegetables. Bake in 350° oven about 20 minutes. Garnish with chopped parsley. Serves 4.

Brenda Hippard, *San Rafael, California*

WILD RICE CASSEROLE

½ cup wild rice
5 ounces water
1 pound hamburger
½ cup chopped celery
½ cup chopped onion
½ cup chopped pepper
1 can chicken rice soup
1 (4-ounce) can mushroom pieces
2 ounces soy sauce

Add water to wild rice. Bring to a boil. Cover and remove from heat. Let stand until all the water is absorbed. Break apart hamburger, and add with all other ingredients to the rice. Mix well (it will be watery). Place in 3-quart casserole; cover and bake at 375° for 2 hours. Stir twice during baking, and remove cover for the last ½ hour. Serves 4 to 6.

Gretchen P. Arthur, *Canoga Park, California*

WILD RICE DINNER

1 pound ground beef
1 tablespoon shortening
2 cups diced celery
½ cup diced onions
½ cup chopped green peppers
1 or 2 cans stewed tomatoes or
  tomato sauce
1 (7-ounce) can mushroom buttons
  or pieces
¾ cup raw wild rice
1 tablespoon salt
¼ teaspoon black cracked pepper
1 can mushroom soup
1 cup unblanched or blanched
  almonds
1 tablespoon butter

Sauté ground beef in shortening. Mix with celery, onions, green peppers, stewed tomatoes, mushrooms and wild rice which has been cooked for 20 minutes and drained. Add 1 tablespoon salt and pepper. Cook in large kettle with trivet in the bottom or on asbestos pad under the pan to keep from burning the contents. Cook for 45 minutes on medium heat. Keep kettle covered. Stir several times with a fork. Bring to a boil 1 can mushroom soup with ½ can cold water or milk. Place 1 cup slivered almonds in 1 tablespoon butter and heat over hot fire until nicely browned. Cover each serving with mushroom sauce and garnish with browned almonds. Serves 4.

Andrew Wilson, *Lakeland, Minnesota*

HARVEST-TIME CASSEROLE

1 head cabbage, shredded (6 cups)
1 teaspoon salt
12 soda crackers
1 cup milk
½ pound bacon, fried or broiled until crisp
2 cups barbecue-flavored potato chips, crushed
1 tablespoon butter
½ cup brown sugar
1 tablespoon flour
2 medium McIntosh apples
1 package smoked sausages

Cook shredded cabbage in small amount of boiling water 5 to 10 minutes, until cabbage is limp but not completely cooked. Stir occasionally to assure even cooking. Add salt. Place half of cabbage in bottom of 2-quart casserole. Sprinkle crushed crackers over top of cabbage. Pour on ½ cup milk. Add layer of crushed bacon. Place remainder of salted cabbage in the casserole. Add remaining ½ cup milk. Sprinkle crushed potato chips over the top. Cream butter, brown sugar and flour; mix with cored and diced apple. Distribute on top of cabbage. Arrange smoked sausages on top of casserole and bake, covered, in 375° oven for 45 minutes. Remove cover for an additional 15 minutes. Serves 4.

Mary E. Scott, *Central Lake, Michigan*

SWEDISH MEATBALL STEW

1 pound ground pork (not pork sausage)
2 slices bread, crumbled
1 egg
1 package onion soup mix
Scant ¼ teaspoon allspice
¼ to ½ cup milk
1 can chicken broth plus ½ can water
3 large carrots
2 medium potatoes
1 medium head cabbage

Mix first 5 ingredients together, adding milk slowly until soft but not sloppy. Roll into small balls and brown gently in a 5-quart Dutch oven or large pan. Pour can of chicken broth over meatballs. Scrub carrots and cut diagonally into chunks. Peel and cut 2 potatoes into chunks. Add vegetables to meatballs and simmer gently for ½ hour. Chop cabbage into large chunks and add. Simmer together until cabbage is just barely fork tender. If desired, broth may be thickened slightly by mixing 1 tablespoon flour in ¼ cup water. Shake in plastic shaker and add to mixture, stirring for at least 5 minutes. Serves 4.

Mrs. Helen Woods, *Santa Monica, California*

POULTRY
For the Birdwatchers

"Granted, Frank Perdue feeds us well but have you ever asked yourself 'why'?"

SPIT-ROASTED WILD MALLARD DUCK
By Roy Andries de Groot

Make the Chinese rubbing sauce the day before by combining in a small pan: 2 tablespoons peanut oil, 2 crushed garlic cloves, 1 tablespoon finely minced red onion, 1 whole star anise, and ½ teaspoon Szechwan pepper. Sauté 1 minute. Add: 2 tablespoons dry Spanish sherry, 2 tablespoons Japanese Shoyu sauce, 1 teaspoon granulated sugar. Stir and boil for 2 minutes. Remove from fire, blend in: 2 tablespoons dark buckwheat honey, 3 tablespoons Chinese Hoisin sauce. Bottle in screw-top jar. Rub this sauce thoroughly over each duck. (Average bird serves 2 people.) Inside each duck place 1 quartered orange. Wrap entire bird with Greek vine leaves, then with fairly thick slices of dark-smoked bacon. Wrap tightly with heavy foil. Roast, turning continuously over very hot fire, for 30 to 40 minutes. Discard wrappings, and brown skin over hottest part of fire. Serve, sprinkled with lemon juice.

GREEK ROASTED EGGPLANT

Press into 2 dozen ¼-inch by ½-inch slits in outer skin a little salt and pepper, a smidgen of rosemary, parsley and a clove of garlic. Foil wrap and roast until the eggplant feels soft when squeezed.

ROAST CHICKEN

The following recipe employs one of the great principles of Southern cuisine: overcook. But it avoids overcal. Scout around your area and see if you can find a place where they sell fresh chickens, or barring that, chickens that have been kept on ice rather than frozen. The difference in taste is amazing. Although an old bird—hen—is more flavorful than a young—fryer—(Escoffier is in agreement with this) the old bird is tougher, and tougher to deal with.

Melt ¾ stick of butter with salt, pepper and ¼ teaspoon dry mustard. Use for basting during cooking. Roast 45 to 50 minutes at 350°.

This may be served warm with a gravy—clear and uncaloric—or with a green mayonnaise if served cold. The clear gravy may be made by boiling the chicken neck and gizzard (but not the liver) over low heat and with barely a cup of water for a long period, tasting as you go, with a little salt and fresh cracked pepper. After the first boil, add two or three segments of tangerine, half a carrot—sliced—a few celery tops and a few onion tops. Taste and season and before serving with long grain rice that has not been washed, add a little of the darker pan drippings from the roast chicken.

CHEESY-CHICKEN MANICOTTI

2 pounds chicken breasts, skinned, boned and quartered
1 tablespoon margarine
1 (5¾-ounce) can mushroom steak sauce
1 cup water
½ teaspoon salt
1 (32-ounce) jar meat-flavored spaghetti sauce (reserve 2 tablespoons)
1/8 teaspoon dried crushed red pepper
¼ cup Italian-style flavored bread crumbs
4 ounces shredded mozzarella cheese
1 tablespoon currants
12 uncooked manicotti shells
2 teaspoons grated, sharp, Italian Romano cheese

Melt margarine in a 10-inch skillet. Add mushroom steak sauce, water and salt and stir until blended. Add chicken pieces, loosely cover and cook at 325° for 10 minutes. Remove chicken pieces only. Set aside to cool. Add the spaghetti sauce and the crushed red pepper to mixture in skillet. Heat until hot. Set aside. Heat oven to 400°. When chicken is cool, dice to ½-inch pieces. Combine diced chicken with bread crumbs, mozzarella cheese, currants and the 2 tablespoons reserved spaghetti sauce in medium-size bowl. Spread 1 cup of hot sauce from frying pan into a 15-by-10-by-2-inch shallow baking dish. Fill uncooked manicotti shells, at largest opening, with chicken filling, about ¼ cup filling to each manicotti shell. Place filled shells in baking dish. Top with the remaining sauce from skillet. Cover with foil, crimping edges well. Bake in preheated oven at 400° for 40 minutes, on first oven shelf from bottom. When done sprinkle with the grated cheese. Serves 4.

(Mrs.) Gloria Dutrumble, *Uncasville, Connecticut*

CHICKEN AND WATER CHESTNUTS

4 medium-size potatoes (white)
2 bunches spinach
½ pound Monterey Jack cheese
10 water chestnuts
1 cup leftover chicken pieces
Pinch of thyme
Salt and pepper

Peel potatoes, dice, boil until tender in water just barely to cover. Mash potatoes in leftover water. Set aside. Blanch spinach in salted water, drain. Butter deep casserole dish. Put in layer of mashed potatoes, layer of sliced cheese, layer of water chestnuts, layer of chicken, layer of spinach. Sprinkle pinch of thyme over spinach and repeat, ending with a layer of cheese on top. Cover casserole and bake 15 to 20 minutes in 350° oven, until cheese has thoroughly melted. Serves 4.

Michelle Holden, *Laguna Beach, California*

CHICKEN CASSEROLE

2 cans chicken noodle soup
1 can mushroom soup
2 eggs
1 package of Stove Top stuffing
(prepared according to package
directions)

2 cooked chicken breasts, cubed
¾ stick margarine, melted
½ cup of crushed cornflakes mixed
with the remaining ¼ stick of
margarine

Mix the first 6 ingredients and place in a buttered casserole. Top with the cornflake mixture and bake in a 350° oven for 1 hour. Serves 4.

Mrs. A.R. Schultz, *Redlands, California*

CHICKEN EL CAPITAN

1 (4- to 5-pound) stewing hen,
cut up
1 can condensed cream of chicken
soup
2 teaspoons salt
½ teaspoon pepper
1 tablespoon lemon juice

2 tablespoons minced onion
½ cup chopped asparagus
6 pitted ripe olives, chopped
½ cup chopped celery
2 tablespoons flour
2 cups milk

Wash and prepare chicken pieces. Cover with cold water and cook on top of stove about 30 to 45 minutes. When tender enough, remove chicken meat from bones, place chicken meat in 2-quart casserole and add soup, salt and pepper. Stir until smooth. Add lemon juice, onion, asparagus, olives and celery. Cook until vegetables are tender, about 30 minutes. Add flour and milk, stirring until smooth and desired thickness for sauce. Heat until bubbly. Serves 6.

Mary Garner, *St. Petersburg, Florida*

CREOLE COUNTRY BAKE

2 pounds chicken breasts
1/3 cup flour
1/3 cup butter or margarine
2 pounds cleaned shrimp

(thaw if frozen)
1 (20-ounce) package frozen mixed
vegetables, thawed

Sauce Ingredients:

½ cup dry white wine—Sauterne
2 cups canned tomatoes
¼ teaspoon celery seed
¼ teaspoon hot sauce

2 teaspoons salt
½ teaspoon oregano
1 clove garlic, chopped fine

Skin chicken breasts and remove meat from bones; cut into 1½-inch cubes. Dredge meat chunks with flour. Heat butter or margarine in heavy skillet; brown chicken cubes until golden. Place meat in a 4-quart casserole; add shrimp and mixed vegetables, tossing lightly to mix. Add all sauce ingredients to drippings in skillet. Heat, scraping up browned bits from bottom of the pan. When mixture begins to bubble around the edges, pour sauce over ingredients in casserole. Cover casserole tightly and bake in preheated 350° oven for 45 to 50 minutes or until shrimp and chicken are tender. Serve with hot steamed rice. Serves 6 to 8.

Mrs. Selma Albrecht, *Minneapolis, Minnesota*

CHICKEN-HEARTED RICE

¾ pound chicken livers
½ teaspoon salt
1/8 teaspoon pepper
¼ cup flour
3 tablespoons cooking oil
1 large onion, sliced
1 green pepper (small), chopped
1 cup raw rice

2 cups well-seasoned chicken
   bouillon
2 tablespoons minced fresh parsley
1 (2-ounce) jar pimiento, drained
1 (4-ounce) can mushrooms,
   drained
¼ teaspoon garlic powder
Salt and pepper to taste

Rinse chicken livers in cold water, trim off fat, pat dry. Combine the ½ teaspoon salt and 1/8 teaspoon pepper with flour in bag. Shake chicken livers in flour. In Dutch oven or electric skillet heat oil, and brown chicken livers over medium-high heat; add onions and green pepper; lower heat. Stir occasionally, and cook until onion and peppers are wilted but not brown (about 5 minutes). Add rice and sauté 2 to 3 minutes. Add bouillon and remaining ingredients; salt and pepper to taste. Cover and cook on low heat 25 to 30 minutes. Serves 4.

Betty Hardy, *Seattle, Washington*

CHICKEN IN THE PINK

2 broiler-fryer chickens,
   cut up into parts and skinned.
   Split breasts in two.
1 can whole cranberry sauce
1 tablespoon minced onion
½ teaspoon salt

¼ teaspoon pepper
½ teaspoon garlic salt
3 tablespoons salad oil
1 (8-ounce) can tomato sauce
2 tablespoons tomato catsup
¼ cup orange juice

Mix together all ingredients except chicken. Place mixture over medium heat to melt cranberry sauce. Cover a 13-by-9-inch baking pan with aluminum foil. Lay chicken pieces on foil. Use only breast halves, thighs, legs and wings. Pour sauce evenly over chicken parts. Bake in a 400° oven for 45 minutes or until fork tender. Serves 6.

Mrs. William B. Castenholz, Jr., *Norwich, Connecticut*

CHICKEN LIVERS MEXICALI

1 pound chicken livers
2 tablespoons flour
1 tablespoon cornmeal
1 teaspoon seasoned salt
½ teaspoon seasoned pepper
3 tablespoons cooking oil
1 package Lawry's enchilada

   sauce mix
1 can tomato sauce
2 cups water
1 (4-ounce) can mushroom stems
   and pieces
½ cup chopped ripe olives

Wash and dry chicken livers. Combine flour, cornmeal, salt, pepper, and shake chicken livers in this mixture until well coated. Heat cooking oil in heavy skillet, add livers and cook over medium heat until lightly browned. Pour off excess oil, and set aside. Combine enchilada sauce mix, tomato sauce, water, mushrooms, and chopped olives. Pour over chicken livers. Cover and cook over low heat 8 to 10 minutes. Serve with fluffy white rice. Sprinkle with grated sharp cheese, if desired. Serves 4.

Mrs. Nan Dixon, *Grass Valley, California*

EARTHEN BIDDY

1 large baking hen
1 can chicken vegetable soup
¼ cup water
1 can tomato sauce
3 medium potatoes
3 medium onions
3 carrots

1 pepper
1 package flat noodles
1 can cheddar cheese soup
Garlic salt
Pepper
Herb seasoning

74

Divide hen into sections. Brown lightly in cast iron pot in a minimum amount of cooking oil. Lightly sprinkle with garlic salt and herb seasoning. Remove from stove and drain. Heat oven to 450°. In an earthen casserole, place ½ can chicken vegetable soup; ¼ cup water; ½ can tomato sauce; 1 sliced potato; 1 sliced onion; 1 carrot; ½ pepper; ½ package flat noodles. Place sectioned and browned hen over mixture. Cover hen with ½ can cheddar cheese soup and remaining noodles. Top with 2 sliced onions, 2 sliced potatoes, 2 sliced carrots and ½ pepper. Sprinkle with garlic salt, pepper, and herb seasoning. Spread ½ can tomato sauce over entire casserole. Cover and place in oven. Cook 25 minutes at 450°. Reduce heat to 250° and cook for 50 minutes. Turn oven off and leave covered casserole in warm oven for 20 minutes. Remove and serve. Serves 6.

Mrs. Lee Newsom, *Jacksonville, Florida*

18-CARROT CHICKEN

5 pounds chicken
2 tablespoons vegetable oil
5 or 6 medium-size carrots
2 oranges
1 small can mushrooms
stems and pieces

Salt and pepper
2 tablespoons parsley flakes
1 teaspoon sugar
1 large cooking pot
with tight-fitting lid

In the cooking pot, brown chicken on all sides in the oil. Meanwhile, peel carrots and slice in circles. Peel 1½ of the oranges (leaving peeling on ½ of 1 orange) and cut both oranges widthwise in ¼-inch slices. Drain mushrooms. When chicken is brown, reduce heat to low, salt and pepper well, then scatter over the chicken in the pot the carrots, oranges, parsley flakes and mushrooms. Add a few drops of water and cover tightly. Cook chicken slowly for about 1 hour, or until it begins to fall from bone. Peek now and then to make sure it's not burning and add small amount of water if necessary; it should steam in existing juices, not boil. When done, remove chicken from pot and add ½ cup water and the sugar to remaining ingredients and let it simmer while you remove the meat from the bones and return it to the sauce. Sauce may be thickened slightly with cornstarch paste if desired. Serves 6.

E. Elaine Eastman, *Fort Collins, Colorado*

FARE GAME IN CABBAGE ROLL

4 Cornish game hens
  (or quail, partridge or squab)
4 cups shredded cabbage
4 small carrots, thinly sliced
4 slices bacon, cut in 1-inch pieces,
  crisply fried and drained
2 tablespoons butter or margarine,
melted
¼ teaspoon caraway seed
16 cabbage leaves
1 cup chicken broth
½ teaspoon crushed tarragon leaves
¼ teaspoon thyme

Preheat oven to 350°. Sprinkle birds inside and out with salt and pepper to suit taste. Combine next 5 ingredients; spoon a fourth into each cavity of birds. Wrap each bird in 4 cabbage leaves; secure with string. Place birds in deep casserole; add remaining ingredients and cover. Bake 45 to 60 minutes or until tender. Remove string and cabbage leaves. Serve with pan juices. Makes 4 servings.

Mrs. Lucille Bredy, *Homedale, Idaho*

MOZZARELLA CHICKEN AND LINGUINE CASSEROLE

3 gloves crushed garlic
1 tablespoon salad oil
1 to 2 pounds boneless chicken
1 pound linguine
16 ounces tomato sauce
¼ cup hot water
4 ounces sliced, drained
  mushrooms
Salt and pepper
4 ounces mozzarella cheese

Brown garlic in hot oil. Cook chicken 3 minutes on each side in oil. Cook linguine. Wash and drain it. Mix tomato sauce, hot water and mushrooms in a bowl. Salt and pepper to taste. Add the following to casserole dish: 1/3 sauce mixture, drained linguine, 1/3 sauce mixture, chicken, sauce mixture, mozzarella cheese. Bake in oven 20 to 25 minutes at 325°. Serves 6.

Rosalyn Segal, *Cambridge, Massachusetts*

THOROUGHLY MODERN CHICKEN LIVERS

2 pounds chicken livers
2 cups mushroom caps (large)
1 pineapple, peeled, cored,
   cut in half, each half to be cut
   in 16 wedges
1 cup chicken bouillon

2 tablespoons soy sauce
2 tablespoons salad oil
2 tablespoons lemon juice
½ teaspoon garlic powder
1 tablespoon sugar

Slice mushroom caps and chicken livers in half. Alternately lay chicken livers, mushroom caps and pineapple wedges on bottom of 2-quart oven-proof casserole dish. Combine chicken bouillon, soy sauce, salad oil, lemon juice, garlic powder and sugar. Pour over each layer of chicken, mushrooms and pineapple. Bake at 350° for 10 to 12 minutes. Serves 4.

Ensign Richard O'Brien, *Detroit, Michigan*

TIJUANA POLENTA

1 cup yellow cornmeal
1 cup cold water
4 chicken bouillon cubes
3 cups hot water
Butter or margarine to grease
   casserole

2 cups cold cooked chicken, cubed
1 (6-ounce) bottle hot taco sauce
3 cups hot half-and-half
½ pound Monterey Jack cheese,
   shredded

Stir the cornmeal into the cold water. Dissolve the bouillon cubes in the hot water and add the wet cornmeal. Cook, stirring constantly, until it draws away from the side of the pan. Butter a deep casserole or baking pan. Spread the polenta (cooked cornmeal) in the casserole. Sprinkle in the cold chicken cubes; pour on the sauce, then the cream. Lastly, sprinkle the cheese over all. Bake at 350° about 45 minutes, or until the cheese is melted and slightly brown. Use as a main dish. Serves 6.

Avis M. Alishouse, *Akron, Colorado*

"How did you enjoy your dinner, sir?"

CHICK-'N-CHILADAS

1 clove garlic, minced
2 tablespoons salad oil
1 (12-ounce) can tomatoes
  (1½ cups)
2 cups chopped onion
2 (4-ounce) cans mild green chilis,
  seeded and chopped
1 teaspoon garlic salt

½ teaspoon oregano
½ cup water
3 cups bite-size cooked chicken
2 cups grated Monterey Jack cheese
2 cups sour cream
1/3 cup shortening
1 package corn tortillas (15)

Cook garlic in salad oil until tender. Add tomatoes, onion, green chilis, garlic salt, oregano and ½ cup water. Cook over low heat until thickened. Combine chicken, cheese and sour cream; mix. Heat shortening. Dip tortillas just enough to make limp; drain. Fill tortillas with chicken mixture; roll up. Place open side down in baking dish. Spoon tomato mixture over top. Bake at 325° for 15 minutes or until hot through. Makes 15.

Joel Allard, *San Antonio, Texas*

CORNISH CASSEROLE

4 Cornish hens
2 cups bread crumbs
4 teaspoons dried salad herbs
½ teaspoon salt
¼ teaspoon pepper
1½ cups Sauterne wine

½ pint sour cream
1 (4-ounce) can mushroom bits
  and pieces, drained
1 (16-ounce) can boiled onions,
  drained
½ cup melted butter

Cut each hen in half and wipe dry. Combine bread crumbs, herbs, salt and pepper. Dip hens into wine and then coat with bread crumb mix. Place on wax paper. Combine wine, sour cream and remaining crumb mixture. Grease a 2- to 3-quart baking dish. Spoon crumb mixture into dish and spread around. Cover with mushrooms and onions. Place hens on top of ingredients and pour melted butter over all. Bake at 350° for 60 to 70 minutes or until hens are tender. Serves 4.

Mrs. Marilyn Uhl, *Clyde, Ohio*

BREASTS OF CHICKEN VICHYSSOISE

3 whole broiler-fryer
  chicken breasts, halved
½ teaspoon salt
½ cup pancake mix
½ teaspoon garlic salt

¼ cup margarine, melted
1 (13-ounce) can vichyssoise soup
1 tablespoon freeze-dried chives
¼ cup Sauterne wine

Sprinkle chicken breasts with salt. Put pancake mix and garlic salt into a small plastic bag and shake chicken pieces in it to coat. Melt the margarine in a casserole or baking dish large enough to hold chicken in a single layer, and roll the skin side of the chicken in it to coat; then turn pieces skin side up. Bake at 425° until chicken is lightly browned. Mix together soup, chives and wine and pour over chicken. Cover and bake at 350° for about 35 minutes, or until chicken is fork tender. Serves 3 to 6.

Georgia Dotson, *Washington, D.C.*

CHICKEN PETIT

1 large onion
1 clove garlic
3 tablespoons cooking oil
4 cooked chicken breasts, each in quarters
1 cup white rice
1 cup water
1 (15-ounce) can dark red kidney beans
½ packet of taco seasoning
2 ounces cream of coconut

Sauté onion and 1 sliced garlic clove in cooking oil. Quickly stir-fry chicken in 12-inch skillet; brown lightly. Remove chicken to platter. Add to remaining onion and garlic in skillet 1 cup rice, 1 cup water and can of kidney beans plus taco seasoning. Cover tightly and cook over low heat for approximately 20 minutes. After 10 minutes you may need additional small amount of water (or white wine). When rice is almost ready, add diced chicken and coconut cream to skillet. Cover and cook additional 10 minutes. Serve piping hot with green salad and corn bread. Serves 6.

Mrs. Marianne J. Whitney, *New City, New York*

CHICKEN SUPERB

1 plump fryer, cut into pieces, or 5 plump chicken breasts
1 teaspoon salt
4 tablespoons butter
1½ cups seasoned poultry stuffing
1 (10-ounce) can condensed cream of mushroom soup
½ cup sliced mushrooms
½ cup sliced, pitted black olives
1 small jar sliced pimientos
½ cup chicken broth
1 (16-ounce) can French-style green beans

Place chicken pieces in small saucepan. Cover with water; add salt and 2 tablespoons butter. Simmer until meat is tender. Remove from heat; cut from bones and chop into large cubes. Place in 1½-quart casserole. Add 2/3 cup of stuffing, mushroom soup, mushrooms, olives, and pimientos. Pour chicken broth over mixture and toss lightly. Add beans and toss again, mixing ingredients well. Sprinkle remaining stuffing over top. Place thin pats of remaining butter over top of stuffing. Sprinkle liberally with water. Bake in 350° oven for 30 minutes, or until casserole begins to bubble. Garnish with parsley. Serves 6 to 8.

Susan Gibson Rainey, *Weldon, North Carolina*

NANA'S CHICKEN

1 (2¼- to 3¼-pound) quartered chicken
¼ cup flour
½ teaspoon salt
¼ teaspoon pepper
1 teaspoon paprika
¼ cup butter
1 cup cream of chicken soup
1 (3- or 4-ounce) can sliced, undrained mushrooms
1 tablespoon sherry

Combine flour, salt, pepper and paprika. Place in bag with chicken and shake to coat. Melt butter in shallow casserole. Add chicken (skin-side down). Bake in 400° oven for 30 minutes. Turn chicken. Combine and heat chicken soup, mushrooms and sherry. Pour over chicken and bake 15 to 30 minutes longer, or until tender. Yield: 4 servings.

Mrs. June Eberbach, *Indianapolis, Indiana*

FISH

The Ones That Didn't Get Away

"What's for dinner?"

SEAFOOD WITH A SOUTHERN ACCENT
By George Rector

Southern seafood traditions will bear a good deal of investigating all right. New England and Louisiana have had plenty of play from itinerant epicures, but there is a long stretch of seashore and imaginative cookery in between. Maryland terrapin, for instance, is adequately famous, but few outsiders have ever experienced what a Carolina cook can do with a "slider"—the local name for ordinary turtle—and I never yet met anybody who had ever heard of, let alone experimented with, the Florida cracker's habit of eating the weird animals which inhabit conch shells. We don't even have to move outside Charleston to find another rib-sticking version of an easily available shellfish. Did you ever have a Carolina shrimp pie?

It isn't a pie at all, being totally innocent of crust, but there's never any point in being pedantic. Fresh shrimp, boiled and shucked, is the best possible beginning, but good canned shrimp will do all right. Two pounds will work out to feed four people to the danger point. If the shrimps are big, cut them in two. Then chop up a small onion and fry it light brown in two tablespoons of butter in a frying pan along with a chopped-up green pepper. Crumble three slices of stale white bread into an ordinary-sized can of tomatoes, mix in the shrimps, all pink and innocent, season them discreetly with pepper and salt and two tablespoons of chili sauce, and then introduce the whole into the frying pan, to be cooked slowly along with the onion for twenty minutes. Three hard-cooked eggs pretty well chopped up join the party at this point, and then everything is poured into a greased baking dish, covered with fine dry bread crumbs, dotted with butter for a richener and softener. Fifteen minutes in a moderate oven will brown the crumbs and produce a magnificent swamp of mingled this and that underneath. It's as rich as the mud in a Sea Island rice plantation, and illustrates the why of the local proverb that Charleston lives on tourists in the winter and shrimps in the summer. With minor variations for stepping the liquid content either up or down, the same layout will do equally well for oysters, crab meat, lobster meat, scallops, and so forth.

HOW TO MAKE A DOWN-EAST LOBSTER STEW
By Samuel T. Williamson

Boil two one-pound lobsters, preferably female, for fifteen minutes. Slit the lobsters open on a flat pan so as to save the juice. Remove tomalley, any coral roe and all meat, including that from the big claws. Squeeze juice from each small claw. Put meat, juice, tomalley and roe in a pan with one-third cup of melted butter. Stir so that each piece is buttered, cover and let stand for about four hours. Heat a quart and a half of light cream in a double boiler to just below the scalding point, then add buttered lobster meat and juice, a quarter teaspoon of sodium glutamate, one teaspoon Maggi liquid flavoring, and, if extra coloring is wanted, a quarter teaspoon of paprika. If necessary, salt to taste, although in most cases the butter and salty juice should be sufficient. When the mixture is cool, put in refrigerator for at least twenty-four hours. Reheat before serving, adding a couple of tablespoons of sherry if desired. Serves six.

OUTDOOR OYSTER ROAST
By Roy Andries de Groot

This requires a large, flat, open, iron pan, balanced over the fire. (I use a Spanish paella, 18 inches across.) Since "roasting" is very quick, first prepare all ingredients. Scrub and wash 3 dozen oysters, or more. Melt, in smallish iron pan, ½ pound butter and keep lukewarm. Coarsely grate ½ cup shelled pecans. Get large open pan spitting hot. Quickly lay on oysters, hollow shell downward. Cover at once with soaking wet burlap sacking. This involves much hissing and steam. Heat butter until it starts sizzling, add grated pecans and stir until darkish brown, being careful not to let them burn. Then add, in one measure, 2 teaspoons tarragon wine vinegar. Sauce will froth violently. Stir once and remove from fire. After about 4 or 5 minutes, lift edge of burlap covering and, with tongs, remove each oyster that has opened sufficiently for a knife to be inserted. Discard flat top shell and serve oysters, with pecan sauce spooned over each.

CLAMBAKE

Buy sweet and white baking potatoes, a few pounds of yellow onions, 2 or 3 ears of corn and 1 small lobster per person. At the beach, immediately organize hunting forces for razor and surf clams, cherrystones, mussels, bay scallops and crabs. Start surf casting for fish. Above the high-water mark dig a trench 2 feet deep, 3 feet wide and 6 feet long. Line the trench with smooth rocks, fill with dry wood and start the fire about 3½ hours before you wish to eat. To clean clams and mussels, scrub and soak in a bucket of sea water to which have been added several handfuls of flour. Wash potatoes, husk corn and wrap each in foil. Clean lobsters and crabs. Cut cleaned fish into chunks, sandwich between onion slices and foil-wrap. After about 2½ hours when the fire dies down to a white-hot and smokeless bed, cover it with a 6-inch blanket of wet rockweed covered with sackcloth soaked in sea water. Vary and spread assorted food interspersed with onions on the cloth in an even layer. Cover with more wet sackcloth, another 6-inch blanket of wet rockweed and over all place a heavy canvas tarpaulin weighted with stones to seal in the steam. Allow about 1 hour for the cooking. Then unroll the tarpaulin from one end and take out only enough food for the first serving. Serve with melted butter in dipping bowls.

PAN-FRIED TROUT WITH EGGS

Allow ¾ pound trout per serving. Clean (leaving on heads and tails), wash, dry, and lightly coat with cornmeal. Break 8 eggs into bowl, add 1 tablespoon finely cut chives and beat lightly. Melt 5 ounces butter in frying pan and put in trout. Brown on both sides for about 10 minutes, then add salt and pepper. Remove fish to a warm dish. Melt another 5 ounces butter and gently stir in ¾ pint heavy cream. Stir continually until sauce has boiled down to the consistency of light cream. Pour half over fish. Give eggs a final beat, then slosh into pan and scramble over gentle heat. Spoon eggs alongside fish and serve garnished with watercress.

OYSTERS LONGCHAMPS AND OYSTER STEW
By George Rector

It was probably my pride in handling oysters with loving care that helped reconcile me to our fancy oyster dishes at the old place—oysters Longchamps, for instance. It's a fine thing to do with bulk oysters in the home. That remark back there about oysters out of a paper bucket was not intended as a slur on anything or anybody but the soulless restaurateur who tries to fake half-shell service, you understand.

A big frying pan is the first field of action for oysters Longchamps. Melt a couple of tablespoons of butter in it and cook in the butter for a few minutes a couple of small white onions minced fine and a half cup of chopped mushrooms. Then thicken that with a couple of tablespoonfuls of flour by patient degrees to avoid lumps. When the mixture reaches a boil, toss in two tablespoons of sherry, a half teaspoon of salt and a few grains of cayenne—all of which makes a very pretty background for an oyster's rich subtleties. Enter the oysters, a full pint of them, plus a tablespoon of chopped parsley—step down the heat before the oysters are put in. They cook in the mixture for just one minute and then the whole business is poured into a shallow casserole, covered with buttered bread crumbs and baked brown in a moderate oven. In the face of that bland creamy deliciousness, it's hard to maintain that oysters should never be cooked. The same holds good for old-fashioned oyster dressing for roast chicken and roast turkey.

If we must cook oysters, however, I can be blinded and backed into an oyster stew without much trouble. The proper way of making an oyster stew is a sort of elementary education in the cooking of oysters in general.

Don't let an unworthy hankering after richness at all costs trick you into making one of those all-cream stews—hot cream is a fine thing for coffee, as they serve it in Vienna, but for any other purpose, it's always sickly rich. The prescription here is two parts of milk to one of cream—not even half and half. Eight oysters to a portion is adequately generous, to be planted in a saucepan with a quarter cup of the oyster liquor, a dash of cayenne, a pinch of salt and, if you fancy the effect, a generous pinch of celery salt. Bring that to a quick boil and give it just a minute of boiling. Then skim the top and put in the milk-and-cream mixture, which should be hot, but not have been allowed to boil. Turn up the fire and stir a little and, just as it reaches a boil again, throw in a tablespoon of butter. Paprika sprinkles prettily over the top, and the oyster crackers, which should of course be served with the stew, are to be floated and pursued by the spoon, no matter what the book of etiquette says.

SCRAMBLED CLAMS AND EGGPLANT EN CASSEROLE

1 eggplant (about 6 inches long)
½ teaspoon salt
1 (6-ounce) can minced clams
1 cup milk
2 tablespoons minced onion
2 tablespoons butter or margarine
1½ tablespoons flour
2 tablespoons chopped parsley
½ cup boiled mushrooms
1/8 teaspoon garlic powder
1 tablespoon Worcestershire sauce
½ cup soft bread crumbs

Cut peeled eggplant into cubes and boil in small amount of salted water. Drain clams, and add to eggplant. Combine milk and clam liquid. Sauté minced onion in 1 tablespoon butter. Add flour, milk, and clam liquid to saucepan and when sauce boils, add parsley, mushrooms, garlic powder, Worcestershire sauce, clams and eggplant. Bake in greased 1½-quart casserole at 325° for 35 minutes. Sprinkle top with bread crumbs and remaining butter. Serves 4.

Jean S. Bailey, *Saratoga, California*

SHORE AND COUNTRY CLAM PIE

4 (6½-ounce) cans minced sea clams
1 pound fresh mushrooms
3 tablespoons margarine or butter
4 or 5 dashes of pepper
1 teaspoon Worcestershire sauce
1 cup clam liquid
1 cup sour cream
2 tablespoons flour
Pastry for 2-crust 9-inch pie
3 tablespoons clam liquid for pie top

Drain clams, SAVE all liquid. Clean and coarse-chop mushrooms to same size as clam pieces. In 10- or 12-inch covered frying pan, cook chopped mushrooms in margarine. Add pepper and Worcestershire sauce. Remove cover, and cook away most of juice. Reduce heat. In separate pan, boil 1 cup clam liquid down to ½ cup. Add concentrated clam liquid to mushrooms. (Total liquid should appear to be a generous ½ cup when pan is tipped away from mushrooms.) Add sour cream to mushrooms. Add flour to clams and mix. Add floured clams to mushrooms. Stir until thickened and remove from heat. Spoon clam-mushroom filling into pie shell. Cover with well-slashed top crust. Sprinkle the 3 tablespoons clam juice over top crust of unbaked pie. Bake in preheated 450° oven for 10 to 15 minutes. Reduce heat to 400° and bake 30 minutes longer or until pie is golden brown and bubbly. Serves 6.

Mrs. William H. Walsh, *Bay Village, Ohio*

CHANNEL CAT, "SHOW-ME" STYLE

2 channel catfish (1 to 2
   pounds each)
Salt
Pepper
Garlic powder
2 lemons (1 for each fish)
Oregano
Paprika
1 tablespoon butter (per fish)

Place fish on aluminum foil. Sprinkle generously with salt, pepper and garlic powder on each side. Grate the rind of one lemon on each fish. Then squeeze the juice of one lemon on each fish. Add a pinch of oregano and dust on both sides with paprika. Dot with butter. Seal aluminum foil with a drugstore wrap so juices do not leak out. Bake in a 350° oven for 45 minutes to one hour, depending on the size of the fish. Serves 4.

Mrs. Gay Schroer, *St. Peters, Missouri*

COD FISH CASSEROLE

1 package frozen codfish
1 teaspoon seasoned salt
6 servings instant mashed potatoes
½ pound salt pork, diced
1 tablespoon butter
1 medium green pepper, sliced
1 small onion, diced

½ cup celery, sliced
1 can cream of celery soup
 (undiluted)
8 ounces fresh mushrooms, sliced
1 package (8-ounce) cooked
 salad shrimp

Season codfish with salt. Wrap in foil and bake 30 minutes at 350°. Drain excess juice and flake. Set aside. Prepare instant mashed potatoes, making them stiff. Set aside. Fry salt pork which has been diced, until crisp. Drain off grease. Add butter, green papper, onion and celery and cook until onion is clear using medium to low heat. Add celery soup, mushrooms and shrimp. Line 12-inch oval casserole with mashed potatoes. Place fish and shrimp mixture in center. Bake in 400° oven for 15 to 20 minutes (until piping hot). Serve garnished with alternate slices of fresh tomatoes and green peppers. Serves 4 to 6.

Mrs. Cletus A. Bille, *Huron, Ohio*

FISH "BATES" CASSEROLE

2 stalks celery
1 to 2 medium onions
2 pounds fresh or frozen fish fillets
 (cod, flounder, or fillets of your
 choice)
Basic recipe for white sauce (butter,
 flour, milk and seasonings)
½ cup dry white sherry wine

 (optional)
Juice of ½ lemon
Paprika
2 to 3 tablespoons Parmesan cheese
Salt and pepper
½ cup prepared bread stuffing mix
3 tablespoons slivered almonds

Line greased oblong shallow baking dish with diced celery and onions. Use enough to cover bottom of baking dish. Place fillets on top of celery and onions. Spoon white sauce mixture over fillets. If wine is used, add to white sauce. Sprinkle with lemon juice, paprika and Parmesan cheese. Season with salt and pepper. Sprinkle with bread stuffing and almonds. Bake at 350° for 30 to 35 minutes or until fish flakes easily. Serves 6.

Mrs. James C. Bates, *Chamblee, Georgia*

THREE-MINUTE TUNA-SPINACH CASSEROLE

1 (7-ounce) can tuna
1 (10-ounce) package frozen
 chopped spinach, thawed
1/3 cup fine dry bread crumbs
3 tablespoons herb seasoned
 stuffing

1 tablespoon lemon juice
¼ teaspoon salt
½ cup mayonnaise
3 tablespoons Parmesan
 cheese, grated

Combine all ingredients in casserole. Sprinkle with additional cheese. Bake at 350° in preheated oven for 20 to 25 minutes. Serve plain or over cooked rice. Serves 4 to 6.

Mrs. Michael Gutshall, *Totowa, New Jersey*

CRAB CASSEROLE AMANDINE

¼ cup butter
¼ cup chopped green pepper
1 medium large onion (chopped)
4 teaspoons arrowroot
1 cup undiluted evaporated milk
1/3 cup water
½ teaspoon chervil
1 cup sliced celery

4 tablespoons chopped pimiento
1 pound fresh crab meat
2 hard-boiled eggs
½ cup slivered almonds
½ cup potato chips, crushed
½ cup shredded cheddar cheese
Salt and pepper to taste

Melt butter; sauté green pepper and onion until tender. Remove from heat and stir in the arrowroot. Combine milk and 1/3 cup water, add to butter and arrowroot. Return to heat stirring constantly until thick and smooth. Stir in the chervil, celery, pimiento, and crab meat. Chop eggs coarsely and add to crab mixture with toasted slivered almonds. Pour into individual buttered ramekins. Top with potato chips and shredded cheese. Bake in 350° oven for 30 to 35 minutes or until bubbling and cheese is melted. Makes 4 servings.

Mrs. Karen K. Trivers, *Wheaton, Illinois*

85

DEVILED CRAB

1 small onion, minced
3 tablespoons butter or margarine
2 tablespoons flour
1 teaspoon dry mustard
1 cup milk
½ teaspoon salt

¼ teaspoon pepper
2 sprigs parsley, minced
½ teaspoon nutmeg
1 egg beaten
½ cup Italian cheese, grated
1 pound fresh or canned crab

Sauté onion in butter until tender, not brown. Remove pan from heat. Stir in flour and dry mustard. Blend well. Gradually add milk. Stir until smooth. Return pan to heat. Cook sauce, stirring constantly until thick. Add salt and pepper, parsley and nutmeg. Stir a little of the sauce into beaten egg. Add egg to the hot sauce. Return to heat, but remove before sauce boils. Add grated cheese and crab meat. Put in shells or ramekins. Bake in 400° oven for 10 minutes or until brown on top. Serves 4.

Maureen Nunn, *Palos Verdes Peninsula, California*

WONDERFUL, ADAPTABLE CASSEROLE

1 cup sliced celery
½ cup finely julienned green pepper
½ cup chopped onion
1 cup of either crab, tuna
  or chicken, cooked
4 tablespoons butter

1½ teaspoons dry mustard
½ teaspoon white pepper
1 tablespoon lemon juice
1 cup of cream or half and half
½ cup saltine cracker crumbs

Sauté until barely crisp celery, green pepper and chopped onion. Combine all other ingredients and cook over low heat for 3 to 4 minutes. Then add the crisp vegetables. Serve on toast triangles, as fillings for pastry shells, or crepes, on waffles, or as a casserole with rice on the side. Serves 4.

Mrs. Plep J. Aver, *Greybull, Wyoming*

CRAB AND WILD RICE

1 cup wild rice
4 cups boiling water
½ cup butter
3 bay leaves
2/3 pound mushrooms (sliced, fresh or canned)
2 tablespoons onion, chopped
3 tablespoons flour

1½ cups milk
1½ teaspoons salt
Pepper
2/3 pound crabmeat (fresh or canned)
½ pound water chestnuts, sliced
1 cup buttered bread crumbs

86

Place wild rice in deep kettle. Pour boiling water over rice to cover. Allow pan to stand until cooled. Repeat this process three times, for light, fluffy rice. Melt butter in skillet. Add bay leaves, mushrooms and onions and cook until lightly brown. Next add flour, stirring until well blended and flour is brown. Remove from heat. Gradually stir in milk. Add salt and pepper and return to heat. Cook until thick and smooth, stirring constantly. Remove bay leaves. Add rice, crab, water chestnuts and mix all ingredients together well. Place in a buttered casserole. Top mixture with buttered crumbs. Bake at 375°, covered, for 25 minutes. Serves 6.

Ivan C. Peck, *Denver, Colorado*

"Ever try goat's milk?"

DOWN EAST FISH CHOWDER

¼ pound salt pork, diced
2 medium onions, sliced or diced
1 small whole onion
4 cups raw potatoes, cut in small
  pieces
1 cup or more of water
2 to 3 pounds haddock fillets

1 teaspoon salt
¼ teaspoon black pepper
Pinch of thyme
1 quart of whole milk
1 small can evaporated milk
1 to 3 tablespoons butter

87

Fry diced salt pork slowly in large kettle until crisp. Add diced onions and cook slowly until yellowed, not brown. Add potatoes and enough water so that potatoes are covered. Bring to a boil. Place fish (whole pieces) on top of potatoes. Add small, whole, peeled onion and seasonings. Cook slowly until potatoes are tender and fish is cooked through. Do not break up fish. Pour in both kinds of milk and heat through thoroughly. Do not boil. Chowder is best when cooked and left to stand (in refrigerator) for an hour or so. Reheat. Add butter and remove whole onion. Serve with crackers and pickles (pilot crackers and sour cucumber pickles are best). Serves 6.

Mrs. A.C. Archibald, *Eastport, Maine*

SEAFOOD CASSEROLE SUPREME

4 cups cooked brown rice
1 stick butter (¼ pound)
4 large mushrooms, sliced thin
3 large tomatoes, peeled and cut
  in wedges
¼ cup grated onion or
  1 tablespoon dried minced onion
2 cups cooked lobster or crab meat
  or 2 cans of either, rinsed
  and drained
½ teaspoon salt

2 or 3 dashes ground pepper
1 can water chestnuts, sliced
¼ cup slivered almonds
1 teaspoon monosodium glutamate
¼ teaspoon bitters
1 cup heavy cream
2 tablespoons minced parsley or
  1 tablespoon dried parsley
½ cup brandy
¼ pound cooked baby shrimp

Melt butter in large skillet. Add mushrooms; stir and cook for 5 minutes. Stir in tomatoes and onions. Cook for another 5 minutes. Add lobster (or crab), salt, pepper, water chestnuts, slivered almonds, monosodium glutamate and bitters. Stir and cook for 3 minutes. Stir in cream and cook until it bubbles. Add parsley and brandy and remove from heat. Line a 2-quart greased casserole with the cooked rice. Turn in the lobster or crab mixture. Top with the baby shrimp. Bake at 350° for 20 minutes. Serves 8.

Mel Wylie, *Richmond, California*

SCALLOPED OYSTERS

1 medium onion, chopped
½ cup chopped celery
1 clove garlic, chopped
¼ cup butter or margarine
2 cups toasted bread crumbs
1 quart oysters

1 teaspoon salt
1 teaspoon pepper
2 hard-cooked eggs, sliced
1 tablespoon Worcestershire sauce
1 pint milk

Cook onion, celery and garlic in small amount of butter until slightly brown; remove from pan. In baking dish, place a layer of bread crumbs, oysters, onion, celery, and garlic. Sprinkle salt and pepper over contents. Make a second layer of all ingredients, and top entire dish with sliced eggs. Add Worcestershire sauce to milk, and pour milk over entire dish. Place in oven at 325° for half hour, or until juice and milk are absorbed. Serves 10.

Mrs. Russell O. Behrens, *Apalachicola, Florida*

PERCH PIQUANT

2 (1-pound) boxes frozen perch
  (or similar fish)
2 large potatoes, peeled, cooked
  and sliced ¼ inch thick
½ pint sour cream

3 tablespoons prepared horseradish
½ cup mayonnaise
2 tablespoons pickle relish
1 teaspoon minced parsley
Salt and pepper to taste

Preheat oven to 350°. Lightly grease a shallow 2-quart casserole. Place fish and potatoes in casserole and dot sparingly with butter. Bake for 20 minutes. Mix sour cream, horseradish, mayonnaise, pickle relish, parsley, salt and pepper together and pour over fish and potatoes. Bake an additional 10 minutes. Serve while sauce is still bubbling. Serves 8.

Mrs. Beryl D. Ames, *New Orleans, Louisiana*

AHOY CASSEROLE

1 (8-ounce) package egg noodles
3 tablespoons butter or margarine
3 tablespoons flour
1½ cups milk
1 (11-ounce) can cream
  mushroom soup
1 (10-ounce) package frozen peas
1 cup grated cheese

½ teaspoon salt
¼ teaspoon pepper
1½ pounds scallops, fresh or frozen
  (thawed)
1 cup fresh mushrooms, sliced
¼ cup diced celery
2 tablespoons butter or margarine

Cook noodles as directed on package and drain. Melt 3 tablespoons butter in saucepan, stir in flour; add milk gradually, stirring constantly. After milk comes to a boil, blend in undiluted soup, frozen peas, ½ cup cheese and seasonings. Set aside. Sauté scallops, mushrooms and celery in 2 tablespoons butter. Drain and add to cheese sauce. Combine this mixture with noodles. Pour into greased casserole and top with remaining cheese. Bake at 400° for about 25 minutes. Serves 6 to 8.

Mary N. Walker, *Harbor City, California*

SHRIMP OR FISH CREOLE

2½ pounds shrimp (cooked) or fish
  (fresh or frozen tuna, etc.)
2 medium onions, choppsed
1 cup green pepper, finely chopped
1½ cups celery, cut in large pieces
¼ cup bacon drippings or oil
3 cans condensed tomato soup
  (10¾ ounces each)
1 tablespoon vinegar

1/8 teaspoon garlic powder
1 bay leaf
4 teaspoons chili powder
3 dashes Tabasco sauce
2 teaspoon salt
Dash Worcestershire sauce
Dash black pepper
½ to ¾ cup white wine

Sauté onion, green pepper and celery in oil until tender. Add remaining ingredients except fish; simmer 30 minutes. Add shrimp or fish and simmer for 10 to 15 minutes. Serve over hot rice. Serves 10.

David Savidge, *Fair Oaks, California*

DANISH SHRIMP SALAD

3 pounds shrimp, shelled
  and deveined
1 tablespoon shrimp spice
¾ cup mayonnaise
½ cup dairy sour cream
2 tablespoons minced onions
3 tablespoons lemon juice
2 to 3 tablespoons chopped

fresh dill
2 teaspoons salt
¼ teaspoon pepper
3 to 4 drops liquid hot
  pepper seasoning
Greens (romaine or Boston lettuce),
  washed

Cook the shrimp in water to cover with the shrimp spice, 5 to 8 minutes. Cool shrimp in the broth. Mix together mayonnaise, sour cream, onion, lemon juice, dill, salt, pepper and pepper seasoning. Drain shrimp and place in bowl; add dressing and mix well. Chill several hours. To serve, arrange shrimp on bed of greens. Serves 6.

Bess Slagle, *St. Peters, Missouri*

"Good grief! There go the TV dinners too!"

PARTY SHRIMP

2 pounds large shrimp
1 tablespoon lemon juice
3 tablespoons salad oil
¾ cup raw rice
2 tablespoons margarine
¼ cup minced green peppers
¼ cup minced onions

1 teaspoon salt
1/8 teaspoon pepper
1 can condensed tomato soup
1 cup heavy cream
½ cup sherry
½ cup slivered almonds

Cook shrimp in boiling salted water for 5 minutes. Place in 2-quart casserole. Sprinkle with lemon juice, oil. Meanwhile cook rice as package directs. Mix shrimp and rice and chill. Sauté peppers and onions in butter. Mix all ingredients in recipe together, with the exception of the almonds. Bake at 350° for 55 minutes. Top with slivered almonds. Serves 6.

Kay Conrad, *Wayland, Massachusetts*

SWEET-SOUR SHRIMP

1 medium onion, quartered
1 cup celery sliced diagonally
2 tablespoons salad oil
2/3 cup firmly packed brown sugar
2 tablespoons cornstarch
½ teaspoon salt
1/8 teaspoon ginger
1/3 cup vinegar

3 tablespoons soy sauce
1 (6-ounce) can pineapple juice
1¼ cups water
2 cups cubed pineapple
1 pound cooked shrimp
1 green pepper cut into
   1-inch pieces

Sauté onion and celery in hot oil until clear but not brown. Dissolve sugar, cornstarch, salt and ginger in vinegar and soy sauce. Add this mixture plus pineapple juice and water to the vegetables. Cook, stirring constantly until thickened. Add pineapple, shrimp and green pepper. Cover and cook for about 5 minutes. Serve over hot rice. Serves 4 to 6.

Helene Drown, *Rolling Hills, California*

SOLE AND CRAB

1 pint sour cream (2 cups)
3 egg yolks
3 tablespoons lemon juice
   (or white wine)

Salt and pepper
2 pounds filet of sole
1 or 2 packages (6-ounce) frozen crab

Mix sour cream, egg yolks, lemon juice, salt and pepper. Cover bottom of 9-by-13-inch baking dish with thin layer of sour cream mixture. Place layer of sole on sauce, season with salt and pepper. Cover with layer of crab, then second layer of sole. Cover with rest of sour cream mixture. Bake at 350° about 30 minutes or until sole flakes easily. Serves 6.

Mrs. C. N. Christensen, Indiana State Symphony Society, *Indianapolis, Indiana*

BREAD

In Time of Knead

"There it is, Ralph, the high point of our day."

SOUTHERN CORNBREAD
By Mary Alice Sharpe

Cornbread, like the polenta of northern Italy, is hearty, nutritious, cheap. In Italy, the cornmeal is poured slowly into salted boiling water until the water is saturated and a kind of wet cake is made which is served as a base for meatless stews and tomato sauces, and then fried the next morning with cheese for breakfast. In the South, the bread is cooked in the oven rather than on top of the stove and here the principle of overcook is deadly. It should be crusty on the outside of the pan and almost mushy in the center. And it should be eaten so hot butter doesn't stand a chance. Burnt fingers and a smile should be the only memory.

1½ cups white cornmeal
½ cup self-rising flour
2 tablespoons sugar

½ stick butter, melted
2 eggs, slightly beaten
1½ cups buttermilk

Mix cornmeal, flour and sugar. Mix butter, eggs and buttermilk and stir into dry mixture. Bake in greased pan about 20 minutes in preheated 400 to 450° oven.

A piece of cornbread with a bowl of vegetable soup makes an unpretentious winter lunch, with stick-to-the-ribs-rather-than-some-other-area vitality.

HONEY BREAD

Homemade bread baked with honey instead of sugar will remain moist longer. The following recipe is for a fruit loaf that makes an excellent gift or a morning snack with coffee.

1¼ cups sifted all-purpose flour
1 teaspoon salt
½ teaspoon baking soda
2 teaspoons baking powder
1 cup whole wheat flour
2/3 cup honey

1 cup buttermilk
3 tablespoons oil or shortening
2 eggs, well beaten
½ cup raisins or chopped dates
1 cup finely chopped
   walnuts or pecans

Sift the flour again with the salt, soda and baking powder. Add the whole wheat flour. Separately, mix the honey, buttermilk and oil with the beaten eggs. Stir in the dry ingredients. Do not over-stir. Fold in the nuts and the dates or raisins. Spoon the batter into a greased 9-by-5-by-3-inch loaf pan. Bake for 50 to 60 minutes in a 325° (moderate) oven.

POPOVERS

Popovers are as light as milkweed blowing in the wind. They're easy to make and their mystery is in the two oven speeds (though there's no reason to tell anybody that).

2 eggs
1 cup milk
1 cup sifted all-purpose flour

½ teaspoon salt
1 tablespoon salad oil

Mix eggs in bowl with milk, flour and salt. Beat 1½ minutes with electric beater. Add salad oil and beat for ½ minute more. Don't overbeat. Fill 6 to 8 well-greased custard cups or a muffin pan about half full. Bake at 475° for 15 minutes. Reduce heat to 350° and bake 25 to 30 minutes, until browned. Before removing from the oven, prick each popover with a fork to let the steam out. You can stuff these with filling—meat, or cheese sauce, or a mushroom, parsley and almond mixture. By themselves, with butter or margarine, they're unforgettable.

ORANGE-DATE-NUT BREAD

The closer bread is to cake, the better. So say some. Children won't argue. And parents might not if the cake is an orange date nut loaf, full of natural ingredients, yet sweet enough to tempt little teeth away from cavity-making, jaw-breaking candies.

1 package pitted dates
   cut into small pieces
   (about 8 ounces)
2 tablespoons shortening
½ cup fresh orange juice
1 tablespoon grated or shredded
   orange peel
1 egg, beaten

2 cups sifted
   all-purpose flour
1 teaspoon baking powder
1 teaspoon soda
½ teaspoon salt
1/3 cup sugar
½ cup chopped pecans

Put the dates and shortening in a large bowl and pour ½ cup of boiling water over them. When this has cooled, add the orange juice and peeling. Stir in the egg. Sift together flour, baking powder, soda, salt, and sugar. Add to the mixture, stirring until just blended. Add the pecans. Pour into a greased, floured loaf pan, about 8 by 4 inches. Bake at 325° for about an hour. Before turning out of pan, cool for about 10 minutes. This may be stored in foil in the refrigerator.

WAFFLES A LA JOHNSON
By Nunally Johnson

Two cupfuls of flour are mixed in a sifter with two teaspoonfuls of baking powder, a half teaspoonful of baking soda and a pinch of salt. Beat this lovely conglomeration into a batter with milk, using the latter as needed for a fairly thick consistency. Add four tablespoonfuls of melted lard. Toss in an egg and continue to beat until the iron is good and hot.

At the end of five minutes one of the handsomest waffles you ever saw will emerge from this iron and, served with butter, will make another man out of you.

AVOCADO BREAD SUPREME

½ cup shortening
1 cup sugar
2 eggs
1½ cups ripe avocado, mashed
1 teaspoon lime or lemon juice

2 cups sifted all-purpose flour
3 teaspoons baking powder
½ teaspoon salt
1 cup pecans, chopped

Beat shortening and sugar together. Add eggs, avocado, lime or lemon juice, flour, baking powder, salt and pecans, and blend. Pour into greased loaf pan and bake in preheated 375° oven 1 hour and 15 minutes. Yield: 1 loaf.
Mrs. C. D. Crites, *Lancaster, California*

CRANBERRY, BANANA-NUT BREAD

1 cup fresh cranberries, chopped
1 banana, mashed
½ cup chopped walnuts
1½ cups flour
2 teaspoons baking powder

1 teaspoon salt
½ cup sugar
1 egg, beaten
½ cup milk
¼ cup oil

Mix cranberries with banana and nuts. Sift flour, baking powder and salt into bowl; stir in sugar. Add beaten egg, milk, oil and fruit to the dry mixture, stirring until flour has been only moistened. Spoon into 9-by-5-inch greased loaf pan. Bake in 400° preheated oven for 25 minutes. Yield: 1 loaf.
Mrs. Paul Robic, *Spokane, Washington*

BARBARA'S LOAF

1 cup All Bran
1 cup brown sugar
1 cup raisins

1 cup milk
1 teaspoon molasses
1 cup self-rising flour

Mix together All Bran, brown sugar, raisins and milk and soak overnight. The next morning add molasses and self-rising flour and blend. Place in greased 9-by-5-inch loaf pan and bake in 350° oven for one to 1¼ hours. Yield: 1 loaf.
Lizbeth Swan, *Greenock, Scotland*

ZUCCHINI BREAD

1 cup salad oil
2 cups sugar
3 eggs
2 cups peeled,
  shredded zucchini
3 teaspoons vanilla

3 cups flour
1¼ teaspoons salt
1 teaspoon soda
¼ teaspoon baking powder
1 teaspoon cinnamon
½ cup nuts or raisins

Mix oil, sugar, eggs, zucchini and vanilla. Sift together flour, salt, soda, baking powder and cinnamon and add to first mixture. Stir in nuts or raisins until blended. Bake in 2 greased and floured 9-by-5-inch loaf pans in 325° oven for one hour. Yield: 2 loaves.
Virgil Crockett, *Great Barrington, Massachusetts*

SUNRISE-SUNSET LOAF

3/4 cup glacé cherries
1 cup sifted flour
¼ cup ground pecans
¼ cup white seedless raisins

¼ cup brown sugar
3/4 cup margarine
3 eggs

Topping:

½ cup glacé cherries
1½ teaspoons white sugar

Line a 2-pound loaf pan with greased waxed paper. Halve cherries. Sift flour; stir in ground pecans, cherries and white raisins. Cream sugar and margarine until light and fluffy. Add beaten eggs one at a time, beating well after each addition. Fold in dry ingredients. Gently turn mixture into loaf pan. Cover top with glacé cherries and sprinkle with sugar. Bake at 325° for 1½ to 1¾ hours, or until golden brown. Cool. Turn out on a rack.

Sheila Marie Rose O'Brien, *East Lansing, Michigan*

COLONIAL PRUNE BREAD

½ cup chopped prunes,
    cooked and drained
2 cups all-purpose flour, unsifted
1 teaspoon salt
1 teaspoon baking powder
½ cup raw apples,

    peeled and chopped
½ cup chopped nuts
2 beaten eggs
1 tablespoon light molasses
1½ cups milk
½ cup quick oats

Wash prunes and chop fine. Combine flour, salt, baking powder, chopped prunes, apples and chopped nuts. In another bowl combine beaten eggs, molasses and milk. Blend well. Add this liquid mixture to the dry ingredients, stirring to blend well. Add quick oats. Turn into a 9-by-5-inch loaf pan. Bake at 350° for 1 hour. Turn out on wire rack to cool.

Mrs. Vincent Garner, *Valencia, Pennsylvania*

HOLIDAY PUMPKIN BREAD

2 cups (1-pound can) pumpkin
4 eggs
1 cup oil
1/3 cup water
½ to 1 cup dates, chopped

3 1/3 cups flour
3 cups sugar
1 tablespoon pumpkin pie spices
2 teaspoons soda
1½ teaspoons salt

Combine pumpkin, eggs, oil, water and dates; mix well. Sift dry ingredients together. Add pumpkin mixture and blend. Pour into 2 greased and floured 9-by-5-inch loaf pans. Bake at 350° for 70 minutes or until done. Cool. (If desired, glaze with 1 cup powdered sugar and 1 tablespoon milk.) Yield: 2 loaves.

Steve Britton, *Boise, Idaho*

CINNAMON, RAISIN LOAF

1 package active dry yeast	1 tablespoon ground ginger
¼ cup warm water	2 teaspoons grated lemon rind
½ cup lukewarm milk	2/3 cup raisins
1 tablespoon sugar	2 2/3 to 3 cups unbleached flour
1 teaspoon salt	3 tablespoons margarine, melted
1 egg	Cinnamon
1 tablespoon margarine	Brown sugar

96

Dissolve yeast in water in large bowl, adding a pinch of sugar to prove yeast. Stir milk, sugar, salt, egg, margarine, ginger, lemon rind and half the flour into yeast mixture. Mix until smooth. Add raisins and enough flour to make handling easy. Turn onto floured board and knead in only as much of the remaining flour as will knead in easily. Place in greased bowl, turning so that top is also oiled. Cover and let rise until doubled.

Shape into 11-by-17-inch rectangle on very lightly floured board. Spread with melted margarine, shake on cinnamon and sprinkle lightly with brown sugar. Roll up and shape into loaf. Place in oiled pan and let rise, covered, until doubled. Before baking, brush top with melted margarine and sprinkle lightly with brown sugar. Bake at 425° for 25 to 30 minutes. If sugar becomes too brown, cover loaf with foil for remainder of cooking time. Yield: 1 loaf.

Mrs. Dee Stein, *Lincolnwood, Illinois*

"Good morning to you, good morning to you, good morning dear sweetheart, good morning to you."

ARNO'S BREAD

2 packages dry yeast
1/3 cup lukewarm water
2 tablespoons sugar
12 cups unbleached all-purpose
   flour
2 cups milk
2 medium potatoes
   (peeled, boiled and mashed)
2 cups potato water
   (from potatoes above)

3 tablespoons melted shortening
1 tablespoon salt
1 cup pitted dates
½ cup dry apricots
½ cup pitted prunes
1 cup raisins
½ pound margarine, soft
1 cup brown sugar
1 tablespoon cinnamon
1 small jar honey

Dissolve yeast in warm water with 2 tablespoons sugar. Let stand a few minutes. Place 6 cups flour in large mixing bowl. Add yeast mixture, milk, mashed potatoes and potato water. Mix with spoon until batter is soft and bubbly. Cover with dish towel and let rise in warm place until doubled in bulk (about 1 hour).

Add remaining 6 cups of flour, melted shortening and salt. Chop dates, apricots and prunes and add to batter along with raisins. Place dough on floured board and knead for 10 minutes. Place in mixing bowl, cover and let rise again for 1 hour.

Punch down dough and divide into 4 equal parts. Roll each part into a 12-by-16-inch rectangle. Spread with soft margarine and sprinkle with mixture of brown sugar and cinnamon. Drip on honey in a crisscross pattern. Roll up dough, tuck in ends and place in greased bread pans. Cover pans with towel and let rise to top of pans (at least one hour). Bake in preheated 400° oven on middle rack 10 minutes. Reduce heat to 350° and bake 50 minutes longer. Remove bread from oven and turn out of pans onto cooling racks. Wait 20 minutes before cutting. Yield: 4 loaves.

A. R. and Polly Justman, *Fort Walton Beach, Florida*

NO-KNEAD GRANOLA SWEET BREAD

1 quart skimmed milk
1½ cups shortening
3 tablespoons salt
6 eggs
1 cup sugar

3 packages active dry yeast
2 cups granola
2 cups raisins
Flour

Heat milk, shortening and salt on medium burner until shortening melts. Cool slightly. Beat eggs and sugar together in large bowl. Add milk and shortening mixture to eggs, then yeast, granola and raisins. Add flour until dough is slightly thicker than cake batter but thin enough to pour into well-greased bread pans. Fill pans to half full. Using warm setting on oven (not more than 150°), allow bread to rise in oven for 45 minutes. Raise temperature setting to 275° and bake slowly for another 45 minutes or until done. Glaze with powdered sugar thinned with hot water. Cool before slicing. Yield: 5 loaves.

Fran Gorton, *Spokane, Washington*

CONVERTIBLE EVERY DAY WHITE BREAD

9 to 10 cups all-purpose flour, sifted
3 tablespoons sugar
1 tablespoon salt
2 cups very hot water
2 cups cold water
3 packages dry yeast
½ cup vegetable shortening
  or cooking oil

Use glass bread pans or equally heavy material. Place all flour in large bowl. With wooden spoon, press flour up around sides of bowl, leaving a hole or depression in middle of flour.

In a smaller bowl, stir together the sugar, 3 tablespoons flour (taken from large bowl) and salt. Add very hot water and stir smooth. Add cold water and stir smooth. Then add the 3 packages of yeast. Stir, cover and keep warm for about 15 to 20 minutes, until mixture is light and bubbly. Stir and then dump yeast mixture (all at once) into the depression of flour in large bowl. Stirring slowly from bottom, add flour until a soft batter is made. Beat this until it seems smooth, being careful not to use too much flour at this stage. Cover and keep warm for 15 to 20 minutes. Then stir slowly from bottom, adding a bit of flour constantly until you can use your hands to knead all remaining flour, and dough becomes soft and spongy. Place on board and continue kneading until dough does not stick to your hands, about 5 minutes. Grease large bowl and put dough back in bowl. Grease dough and cover. Keep in warm place until doubled in bulk.

Punch down and knead again until soft. Grease and let rise again in bowl until doubled. Always knead on floured board. Punch down again and knead for a few minutes before forming into 3 loaves. Place in well-greased pans and "bathe" loaves with melted shortening. Let rise until doubled, keeping warm. Handle carefully while placing in a preheated oven of 425°. Bake for 30 or 35 minutes. Check after first 15 minutes. If it seems a bit hot, turn back to 375° or 400°. When done, remove from pans and cool on rack. These loaves may be frozen and kept for an indefinite time in freezer. Yield: 3 loaves.

Mrs. Tod S. Chearonn, *Londonville, Ohio*

GRANDMA VOELKER'S COFFEE CAKE

1 cake yeast
1 cup lukewarm water
½ cup lard
1 cup boiling water
1 cup cold water
½ cup sugar
2 to 3 eggs, beaten
1½ teaspoons salt
9 cups flour
  (approximate)

Soak yeast in 1 cup lukewarm water and set aside. Melt lard in 1 cup boiling water. Add cold water, sugar, eggs, salt and yeast to lard mixture. Stir in about 4 cups of flour and beat 3 minutes (as for cake). Work in the remaining flour and keep beating until you have a soft dough. Place in greased bowl and let rise until doubled in bulk. (May be regrigerated overnight, or longer.) Divide dough and place in four 8-inch or 9-inch round cake pans. Brush with melted butter or margarine and sprinkle with a mixture of sugar and cinnamon. Let rise again until doubled. Bake in 350° to 375° oven for 20 to 30 minutes. Yield: 4 coffee cakes.

Mrs. Adolph Voelker, *Tell City, Indiana*

ALMOND ROSE ROLLS

1 package active dry yeast
¼ cup lukewarm water
1/8 cup margarine
1/8 cup vegetable shortening
¼ cup sugar
1 teaspoon salt
1 tablespoon grated lime rind
½ cup scalded milk
½ cup ice water

1 egg, slightly beaten
4 cups presifted all-purpose flour
1/3 cup squeeze liquid margarine
3/4 cup firmly packed
   light brown sugar
2 tablespoons instantized flour
1 teaspoon almond flavoring
1 teaspoon rose extract
Cream

Dissolve yeast in lukewarm water. Combine margarine, shortening, sugar, salt, grated lime rind and scalded milk. Add ice water; cool to lukewarm. Blend in egg and the dissolved yeast. Add flour gradually, mixing well after each addition. Cover and let rise in warm place 45 to 60 minutes.

Combine squeeze liquid margarine, brown sugar, instantized flour, almond and rose extracts and mix well. Reserve as filling for rolls.

Roll dough into two 12-by-10-inch rectangles. Spread with almond rose filling. Roll as for jelly roll and cut into ½ inch slices. Arrange slices on greased baking sheet. Flatten to ¼-inch thickness. Place a blanched almond and preserved rose petals (if available) in center of each roll. Let rise 30 to 45 minutes. Brush tops of rolls lightly with cream. Bake in preheated 400° oven 12 to 15 minutes. Remove immediately from baking sheet. Yield: 2½ dozen.

Mrs. Helen Mize, *High Point, North Carolina*

BUTTERSCOTCH PARTY ROLLS

1 cup evaporated milk
1 cup brown sugar
½ cup butter
1 tablespoon vanilla
4 eggs
2 teaspoons salt

2 packages active dry yeast
½ cup lukewarm water
6 cups white flour
1 cup chopped nuts
2 cups confectioners' sugar

Combine evaporated milk and brown sugar in a saucepan and cook for 5 minutes after mixture has started to boil, stirring constantly. Take off stove and stir in butter and vanilla. Reserve ½ cup of this butterscotch sauce for the filling and frosting. Break eggs into a large mixing bowl and beat well. Add salt, lukewarm butterscotch sauce, and yeast that has been dissolved in the lukewarm water. Add 3 cups flour. Mix together using low speed, then beat at medium speed for 3 minutes. Stir in the remaining flour and half the nuts. Scrape bowl down, cover, and let rise until double in bulk. To the ½ cup reserved butterscotch sauce stir in 2 cups sifted confectioners' sugar.

When the dough is doubled in size, punch down and roll out to an 18-by-24-inch rectangle. Spread half the filling on the dough. Roll up as for a jelly roll, starting with the 24-inch side. Cut in 36 equal pieces. Put in greased muffin tins and top each roll with an equal amount of the remaining filling and nuts. Let rise until double in size. Bake at 375° for 20 minutes, or until golden brown. Yield: 36 rolls.

Marilee Jean Johnson, *Robbinsdale, Minnesota*

FRUIT MUFFINS

1 cake compressed yeast
¼ cup lukewarm water
½ cup old-fashioned oatmeal
½ cup yellow cornmeal
½ cup All Bran
½ cup brown sugar

1 teaspoon salt
1 rounded tablespoon shortening
2 cups boiling water
5 cups white flour
Cooked prunes

Dissolve yeast in lukewarm water. Mix together oatmeal, cornmeal, All Bran, brown sugar, salt and shortening in bowl. Pour on boiling water and let stand until lukewarm. Add yeast mixture and beat a few minutes with spoon. Add 5 cups white flour and knead into soft ball.

Place in greased bowl and let rise until doubled in bulk. Spoon into large muffin pans, filling half full. Make deep hole in center of each muffin and place cooked prune deep in hole. Lightly spread muffin dough with butter and let rise again until doubled. Bake in 350° oven approximately 25 minutes or until golden brown on top. Remove from pans, spread tops with butter and sprinkle with wheat germ.

Mary E. Ralph, *Forsyth, Missouri*

100

SOUR CREAM NUT-FILLED ROLLS

4 cups sifted flour
¼ cup sugar
1½ teaspoons salt
1 cup (2 sticks) margarine
2 yeast cakes or packages of

dry yeast
2 tablespoons sugar
½ cup milk
1 cup sour cream
2 beaten eggs

Cut the margarine into dry ingredients in large bowl, as for pie crust. Make a "well" in center of mixture. Dissolve yeast and sugar in milk. Place in "well" with sour cream and eggs. Stir all ingredients together, using a large spoon to mix, forming a soft dough. Cover with a damp cloth or merely sift a little flour over the top of dough and place bowl of dough in refrigerator to rise overnight. The next morning, roll out half of dough at a time on well-floured board, forming a circle. Cut 12 pie-shaped wedges from each circle. Put a spoonful of nut filling at wide end of each wedge. Roll up, sealing ends as you start by pulling ends of dough up over the nut mixture, then rolling toward point of dough. Let rise in 2 greased 9-by-12-by-2-inch pans, or use two jelly-roll pans, if preferred. When rolls have doubled in size, bake at 350° for 20 to 25 minutes. Soon after taking from the oven, drizzle top with glaze.

Nut Filling:
¾ cup (1 stick) margarine
2 cups walnuts, ground

½ cup sugar
½ teaspoon cinnamon (optional)

Melt margarine in saucepan and add remaining ingredients.

Glaze:
¾ cup confectioners' sugar
1½ tablespoons water
½ teaspoon vanilla

Stir these 3 ingredients together in cup or bowl and drip over the rolls while they are still very warm from the oven.

Joyce H. Orcutt, *Punta Gorda, Florida*

POSTHASTE BARBECUE BREAD

1 cup spaghetti sauce
with mushrooms (use
all mushrooms in can)

1 (13¾-ounce) package hot roll mix
1 egg
½ cup shredded cheddar cheese

Heat spaghetti sauce until warm (not hot). Pour into 3-quart bowl and sprinkle with yeast from packet in roll mix. Stir until dissolved. Add egg and then flour mixture. Blend well. Cover and let rise in warm place until doubled in size, 30 to 45 minutes on top rack of unheated oven. Put large pan of hot water on bottom rack.

On floured surface toss dough lightly until no longer sticky. Shape dough and pat into 10- or 12-inch greased round pan or ovenproof skillet (12-inch pan preferable). Sprinkle top with grated cheese and let rise again in warm place until light and doubled in size, 30 to 45 minutes. Bake in preheated oven at 375° 20 to 25 minutes or until golden brown. Brush top with melted butter or margarine. Yield: 1 loaf.

This bread is shrimp-colored and moist and freezes well.

Mrs. Leon Pruitt, *Winslow, Indiana*

MOD PAD SKILLET BREAD

1 package hot roll mix
3/4 cup very warm water
(105° to 115°)
1 egg
1/3 cup dairy sour cream
3/4 cup pimiento cheese spread

2 teaspoons caraway seed
2 teaspoons freeze-dried
chopped chives
¼ teaspoon soda
3/4 cup potato flakes

Grease 10-inch iron skillet or one with removable handle that isn't all metal. In large bowl, dissolve yeast from hot roll mix in water; stir in egg, sour cream, cheese spread, caraway seed, chives and soda. Add flour mixture and potato flakes; blend well. Cover. Let rise in warm place until light and doubled in size (45 to 60 minutes). Punch dough down and place in prepared skillet. Pat dough out to cover bottom of skillet. Cover. Let rise again in warm place until light and doubled in size (45 to 60 minutes). Bake bread in preheated oven at 375° from 30 to 40 minutes, until golden brown. Remove from pan to cool. Brush top with melted butter or oleo, if desired. Yield: 1 10-inch round loaf.

Otto Davis, *Waynesboro, Mississippi*

QUICK APRICOT/ALMOND BREAD

½ cup granulated sugar
1 egg
1¼ cups apricot nectar

¾ cup roasted chopped almonds
1 cup chopped dried apricots
3 cups biscuit mix

Mix together sugar, egg, apricot nectar, almonds and apricots. Stir in biscuit mix. Pour into well-greased 9-by-5-by-3-inch loaf pan. Bake in preheated 350° oven for 45 to 50 minutes. Remove from pan to rack and cool thoroughly before slicing. Yield: 1 loaf.

Diane M. Haley, *Clearwater, Florida*

EASIEST CHEESE BREAD YET

3¾ cups prepared biscuit mix
1½ cups milk
1 egg, beaten

¾ cup grated sharp cheddar cheese
2 teaspoons caraway seed
1 tablespoon butter

Combine biscuit mix, milk, egg and cheese. Set aside ¼ of batter and add caraway seed and butter. Reserve. Make dough into loaf and put in 9-by-5-inch bread pan. Spread reserved dough with caraway seed and butter on top of loaf. Bake in 350° preheated oven for 1 hour. Yield: l loaf.

Vivian S. Mindrum, *Minneapolis, Minnesota*

COCONUT CHEEREE PUMPKIN BREAD

½ cup vegetable shortening
2 eggs
1/3 cup Jamaica rum
1 cup cooked pumpkin
1 cup ripe crushed bananas
2 cups sifted biscuit mix

1½ cups sugar
½ teaspoon ground cinnamon
½ teaspoon ground nutmeg
½ cup candied cherries, cut up
½ cup coconut, shredded
½ cup chopped mixed nuts

Grease and flour loaf tin (9-by-5-by-3-inch approximately). Mix together in bowl shortening, eggs, rum, pumpkin and bananas. Sift biscuit mix, sugar, cinnamon and nutmeg together. Add to pumpkin-banana mixture and beat until smooth. Fold in cherries, coconut and nuts. Pour into pan and bake at 350° for 1 hour. Yield: 1 loaf.

Mary Garner, *St. Petersburg, Florida*

CAKES & PIES

You've Got Some Crust

"*Now, that's what I call a rum cake.*"

CAKEWALK
By Mary Alice Sharpe

In many homes a special Easter cake is made that is becoming as much a tradition as fruitcake is at Christmas time. It is wholesome enough to be used as bread and toasted, and sweet enough to bring the children running.

1/3 cup warm water
2 packages active dry yeast
1 cup hot milk
½ cup honey
1½ teaspoons salt
1/3 cup butter or margarine
2 eggs, well beaten
4½ cups sifted
  all-purpose flour
1½ cups coarsely chopped pecans

or walnuts
½ cup candied halved cherries
½ cup finely chopped citron
(Candied orange or lemon
peel may be substituted
for the cherries or the citron,
depending on the sweetness
desired. White raisins may also
be used.)

Soften the yeast in water. Mix the hot milk, honey, salt and butter. When the mixture is lukewarm, add half the flour, beating until smooth. Add the yeast, eggs and the rest of the flour. Mix until the dough is moderately stiff. Flour the breadboard just enough to prevent sticking. Knead until dough is smooth. Place in greased bowl, turning so the top will be greased. Cover and let rise until doubled in size (about 1½ hours). Turn onto floured board. Pat dough to ½-inch thickness. Scatter the nuts and fruits over the surface. Fold dough over to enclose and knead with a light touch several times to distribute the fruit. Divide the dough in half. Shape each piece into a ball. Place in two greased, round, oven-proof cake dishes, 8 by 1½ inches. Cover and let rise again until the bulk is doubled (about an hour). Brush with melted butter. Heat oven to 350°. Bake for half an hour or until done. Cool on racks for several minutes. Remove from pans.

You may coat this cake with a sugar icing made from 2 cups sifted confectioners' sugar, 2 tablespoons warm milk, 1 teaspoon of vanilla flavor. Blend together until smooth. Top the cake with designs made of nut meats and cut fruit.

WEDDING CAKE
By Mariea Creamer

2 pounds flour of love
¼ pound good looks
½ pound sweet temper
½ pound buttered youth
1 ounce powdered wit

1 ounce dry humor
2 tablespoons sweet argument
½ pint common sense
½ pint rippling laughter

Put the flour of love, good looks and sweet temper into a home. Beat the butter of youth to a cream. Mix together powdered wit, dry humor and sweet argument and add to the above. Pour in gently common sense and rippling laughter. Stir together until well mixed, then bake at a uniform temperature forever.

This recipe has been handed down in my family and has proven itself.

CAN'T WAIT APPLE CAKE

4 cups apples, diced
½ cup cooking oil
2 cups sugar
2 eggs, well beaten
2 cups flour

1½ teaspoons soda
½ teaspoon salt
1 teaspoon cinnamon
1 teaspoon vanilla
1 cup chopped walnuts

Combine apples, oil and sugar. Add beaten eggs. Sift together flour, soda, salt and cinnamon and add to batter. Stir in vanilla and nuts. Bake in greased 9-by-13-inch pan in 375° oven for about 45 minutes.

Lillian Freedman, *Van Nuys, California*

AUNT BERTHA SANBORN'S BLUEBERRY CAKE

1 3/4 cups flour
2 tablespoons baking powder
Pinch salt
1 cup sugar

¼ cup shortening or butter
1 egg, beaten
3/4 cup milk
1 cup or more floured berries

Sift together flour, baking powder and salt and set aside. Cream together sugar and shortening. Add egg and milk and beat well. Add sifted dry ingredients. Fold floured berries into the batter before the dry ingredients are completely moist and put in greased and lightly floured 9-by-5-inch loaf pan. Bake in preheated 350° oven 40 to 45 minutes or until top is golden brown. Serves 8.

Miss Lynne Ellen Zalesak, *Harwich Port, Massachusetts*

"Did I get him?"

MAPLE BLUEBERRY CAKE WITH LEMON GLAZE

¼ cup shortening
½ cup maple syrup
½ cup brown sugar
3/4 cup sour cream
2 eggs, beaten
3/4 cup blueberries, drained

2 cups flour
1 teaspoon ginger
1 teaspoon baking soda
¼ teaspoon salt
½ cup drained blueberry juice

Heat shortening, syrup, and sugar together in a saucepan. Add sour cream, beaten eggs, and blueberries. Sift dry ingredients, and add to batter. Mix well, and pour in greased 10-inch spring-form pan, or 10-inch bundt pan. Bake in 350° oven for 30 minutes, or until inserted knife comes out dry. After cake cools, pour reserved blueberry juice over the cake (this allows for the cake to become extra moist, before applying the lemon glaze).

Lemon Glaze:

1 tablespoon milk
2 tablespoons lemon juice
¾ cup confectioners' sugar

Gradually blend milk and lemon juice into confectioners' sugar and pour over cake before serving, let glaze set; then slice cake. Serves 10 to 12.
Mrs. Martha Swanson, *Killingworth, Connecticut*

HOLIDAY APPLE CAKE

3 cups chopped peeled baking apples
3/4 cup sugar
3/4 cup golden raisins
1/3 cup chopped almonds
3 tablespoons flour
1 teaspoon cinnamon
2½ cups unsifted flour
2 teaspoons baking powder

1½ teaspoons salt
2 eggs
1/3 cup oil
1/3 cup water
1/3 cup sugar
1½ teaspoons vanilla
Confectioners' sugar frosting

Combine chopped apples, 3/4 cup sugar, raisins, chopped nuts, 3 tablespoons flour and cinnamon. Set aside. Blend the flour, baking powder and salt. Beat together eggs, oil, water, 1/3 cup sugar and vanilla. Gradually stir in flour mixture until completely blended. Turn batter out onto well-floured board; with floured hands shape batter into ball and divide into 3 equal pieces. Roll out one piece to make a 9-inch square. Place it in an oiled 9-inch square baking pan. Cover with half of the apple mixture. Roll out the second piece just as the first piece and place over the apple layer; then cover with remaining apple mixture. Roll out third piece of dough also to 9-inch square and place over second apple layer to form top crust. Make several slits in it to allow the steam to escape. Bake in 350° oven 60 to 70 minutes. While warm frost with confectioners' sugar frosting. Frosting: Mix 1 cup confectioners' sugar with 2 tablespoons milk or water and ¼ teaspoon vanilla extract. Spread on warm cake. Serves 9.
Mrs. E. Duncan, *New Britain, Connecticut*

CARIN' ABOUTCHA CARROT CAKE

2 cups flour
2 teaspoons baking powder
1 teaspoon salt
1½ teaspoons soda
2 teaspoons cinnamon
2 cups sugar

1½ cups oil
4 eggs
2 cups grated carrots
1 (8½-ounce) can crushed pineapple
½ cup chopped nuts

Combine flour, baking powder, salt, soda and cinnamon. Add sugar, oil and eggs. Mix well. Add carrots, drained pineapple and nuts. Bake in 9-by-13-inch greased and floured pan at 350° for 35 to 40 minutes.

Frosting: (Optional)

½ cup butter
1 (8-ounce) package cream cheese
1 teaspoon vanilla

1 pound powdered sugar
Milk

Cream butter, cream cheese and vanilla. Add powdered sugar. If too thick, add milk to spreading consistency. Serves 12.

Lee Craig Douglas, *Los Angeles, California*

AUNT DOROTHY'S CHEESECAKE

13 graham crackers
3 tablespoons butter
1 pound cream cheese

1 cup sugar
3 eggs
1 teaspoon vanilla

Topping

1 pint sour cream
1 tablespoon sugar
½ teaspoon vanilla

Crush graham crackers; combine with butter and line an 8-by-12-inch or an 8-by-8-inch baking dish. Blend cream cheese, sugar, eggs and vanilla. Pour mixture in lining and bake 25 to 35 minutes in 350° preheated oven. Mix sour cream with 1 tablespoon sugar and ½ teaspoon vanilla. Spread this topping on cake after it has cooled. Place in oven at 300° for 5 minutes. Refrigerate overnight.

Mrs. Harry S. Gill, *South Yarmouth, Massachusetts*

CREAM CAKE

4 eggs, separated
1½ cups sugar
½ pint heavy cream

1 teaspoon vanilla
1¾ cups (self-rising)
  cake flour

Beat egg yolks until lemon colored. Add sugar and beat until well combined. Add cream and vanilla and blend at low speed. Add cake flour and mix thoroughly. Beat egg whites until stiff and fold into batter. Pour into greased 9-inch or 10-inch tube pan. Bake in 350° oven for approximately 1 hour.

Mrs. Donald S. Law, *Bradenton, Florida*

LIGHT CHEESECAKE

Cake Crust:

1 cup flour
1 teaspoon double-acting
  baking powder
2 tablespoons sugar
½ teaspoon salt

2 ounces sweet butter
1 egg yolk (reserve the white
  for filling below)
2 tablespoons ice water
2 tablespoons bread crumbs

Sift flour, baking powder, sugar and salt; cut in butter in small pieces and mix lightly. Add beaten egg yolk and ice water, knead 2 minutes, wrap in floured wax paper and chill for 1 hour; roll out to fill buttered round 9-inch baking pan and sprinkle lightly with fine white bread crumbs.

Cheese Filling:

½ pound dairy creamed
  cottage cheese
3 egg yolks
¾ cup sugar
½ pint dairy sour cream
1 teaspoon grated lemon rind

1 teaspoon vanilla extract
1 level tablespoon flour, sifted
1 level tablespoon cornstarch, sifted
4 egg whites
¼ teaspoon cream of tartar

Rub cheese through fine sieve, add 3 egg yolks, sugar, sour cream, lemon rind, vanilla, flour, cornstarch. Blend well. Beat 4 egg whites with cream of tartar until *stiff* peaks are formed; fold carefully into cheese mixture (do not stir) and spoon onto crust; bake in preheated oven at 325° for about 20 minutes; then decrease to 320° and bake another 40 minutes; let cool in draft-free place. (This cake may be successfully reheated the next day without losing any of its flavor and freshness.)

Mrs. Mary Wittman, *Paramus, New Jersey*

ALMOND CREAM CAKE

1 cup blender-grated almond meats
1 cup whole wheat pastry flour
2 teaspoons baking powder
¼ teaspoon salt
3/4 cup soft butter

1 cup sugar
3 eggs (room temperature)
1 teaspoon almond extract
1½ cups hot milk
2 pints whipping cream

Preheat oven to 325°. Grease and flour 2 round cake pans. Combine grated nuts, flour, baking powder, and salt in a mixing bowl. Set aside. Place butter, sugar, eggs, and almond extract in blender and blend on a low speed until contents are of uniform consistency. Gradually add hot milk while blending on lowest speed. Continue blending for 30 seconds on low. Add blender contents to dry ingredients. Mix well until batter looks smooth. Bake for 30 to 45 minutes or until center springs back when lightly touched. Cool cake on rack. Whip cream and sweeten lightly with confectioners' sugar. When layers are completely cooled, pile cream between layers and on top of cake. Garnish with raw slivered almonds and chill before serving. Serves 8.

Carol L. Terrizzi, *Hyde Park, New York*

BICENTENNIAL CHERRY CAKE

1 package sour cream
  chocolate fudge cake mix
1 cup fancy quality applesauce
1 (8-ounce) jar maraschino cherries,
  drained and chopped
1/3 cup maraschino cherry juice
2 eggs
1 cup chopped nuts
  (pecans or walnuts)

Preheat oven to 350°. Blend cake mix with the applesauce, cherry juice and eggs. Use large bowl on low speed until moistened. Scrape bowl constantly. Beat 4 minutes on medium speed; scrape bowl often. Stir in cherries and nuts. Grease oblong 13-by-9-by-2-inch pan and dust with flour. Pour batter into pan. Bake at 350° for 35 to 40 minutes. Cake is done if it springs back when touched lightly in center. Cool 10 minutes.

Frosting

1 can cherry frosting
  (ready to spread)
1 (4-ounce) jar maraschino cherries,
  drained

Spread frosting over cake and decorate with whole cherries. Serves 12.

Edna B. Chadsey, *Corpus Christi, Texas*

ECONOMY DATE CAKE

2 cups chopped dates
1 cup white sugar
1 cup water
½ cup oil
¼ teaspoon salt
½ teaspoon grated cloves
¼ teaspoon nutmeg
¾ teaspoon cinnamon
2 cups flour
½ teaspoon baking powder
1 teaspoon baking soda
¾ cup boiling water

Combine dates, sugar, 1 cup water, oil, salt, cloves, nutmeg and cinnamon in pan and bring to boil. Boil for 3 to 5 minutes. Cool. Sift together flour and baking powder and add to cooled date mixture. Dissolve baking soda in ¾ cup boiling water, add to batter and mix well. Bake in greased 10-by-14-inch Pyrex dish for 1 to 1½ hours at 325°. This cake remains moist and ships well.

Mrs. Kathryn K. Rigney, *Kingston, Ontario, Canada*

HINT OF BRANDY LOAF CAKE

1 stick butter (room temperature)
2/3 cup raw sugar (turbinado)
1¾ cups flour (unbleached white)
1½ teaspoons baking powder
2 eggs
½ cup milk
½ teaspoon brandy flavoring
½ teaspoon vanilla extract

Cream butter, blend in raw sugar, 1/3 cup at a time. Measure in flour, ½ cup at a time, blending; then before last ¼ cup, blend in baking powder. Scrape sides and bottom. Add eggs one at a time. Thoroughly blend in ½ cup milk; then add brandy flavoring, vanilla. Bake at 350° for 1 hour in loaf pan greased and floured with butter or spray coating and confectioners' sugar. Serves 8.

Lorraine P. Stoos, *Denver, Colorado*

CALIFORNIA FRUIT CAKE

Bowl 1:

3 cups candied cherries
  (red and green for Christmas)
3 cups candied pineapple
  (red and green)
2 cups dates

1 cup candied orange peel
1 cup citron
3 cups blanched almonds
3 cups dried apricots

Put the cherries in whole and cut the other fruit the size of the cherries. Cut almonds in half, lengthwise. Sprinkle with flour to separate the sticky fruit. Put 3 cups of dried apricots in a stewing pan with just enough cold water to cover. Cook until tender. Set aside to cool.

Bowl 2:

1½ cups butter
2 cups sugar
4 cups flour

1 teaspoon salt
1 teaspoon lemon rind, grated
8 eggs

Cream sugar and butter. Combine flour, salt and lemon rind. When sugar and butter are very creamy, add flour and eggs, alternating 1 egg at a time. Fold the unbeaten eggs into the mixture, turn it over each time like cream puffs. Next add the fruit from bowl 1. Last add the apricots, folding them in; they will lose their form but will flavor and color the cake. Fill cake pan or any container (even unusually shaped tin cans) almost to the top. The cake will not rise very much. Bake in a very slow oven (275° to 325°) for 1½ hours. Watch the cakes so they do not scorch. These do not have to be made far ahead of time as the cakes are very moist.

Mrs. Gretchen P. Arthur, *Canoga Park, California*

JUMPIN' GIN-GERBREAD CAKE

1 cup butter or margarine
½ cup sugar
4 egg yolks
1 cup molasses
3 cups all-purpose flour

1 teaspoon pumpkin pie spice
¼ teaspoon salt
1½ teaspoons baking soda
1 cup hot gin

Glaze:

1 cup sifted powdered sugar
1 tablespoon gin

1 tablespoon orange juice
1/3 cup slivered almonds

Cream margarine or butter with sugar until light and fluffy. Beat in egg yolks and molasses. Sift flour with spice, salt, and baking soda. Stir into creamed mixture. Add hot gin and mix until smooth. Grease and flour a bundt or 10-inch tube pan. Pour in batter and bake at 350° for 40 to 45 minutes or until a toothpick inserted comes out clean. Cool in pan 10 minutes. Invert on serving dish. Combine powdered sugar, gin and orange juice. Pour over cake and sprinkle with slivered almonds.

Mrs. Phelles Friedenauer, *Rockford, Illinois*

GOOBERITZY CAKE

¼ cup butter or margarine
1 cup sugar
1 teaspoon vanilla extract
½ cup sour cream
2 egg yolks
½ cup flour

2 teaspoons baking powder
½ teaspoon salt
¼ teaspoon baking soda
2 cups finely ground peanut meats
2 egg whites

In large mixing bowl combine butter, sugar, vanilla, sour cream and egg yolks. Using medium speed, beat until smoothly mixed. Sift together flour, baking powder, salt and baking soda and add ground peanuts. Combine dry and creamed mixtures and beat thoroughly. Beat egg whites until stiff but not dry. Fold into cake batter. Pour into two greased and floured 8-inch round cake pans. Bake in 350° oven for 30 to 35 minutes. Cool.

Frosting:

½ pint heavy whipping cream
½ cup sugar
½ teaspoon vanilla extract

Beat cream until stiff. Add sugar and vanilla. Use as filling between layers and for frosting on top and sides. If desired, sprinkle ground peanuts over top.

Mrs. Nan Dixon, *Grass Valley, California*

LEMON LOAF CAKE

2 egg whites
1 teaspoon vanilla
1 cup soft shortening (½ butter)
¾ cup granulated sugar
½ cup brown sugar
2 large egg yolks

2/3 cup milk
1/3 cup water
2 cups flour
¾ teaspoon soda
¾ teaspoon salt
2 tablespoons prepared lemon peel

Beat egg whites until fluffy and peaking; add vanilla and set aside. Cream shortening, sugars and egg yolks. Alternately add liquids and sifted dry ingredients. Fold into egg white mixture together with lemon peel. Pour carefully into two greased loaf pans. Bake at 350° for 30 minutes. Time may vary at different altitudes. Cool on sides. This is best served as cake while warm or sliced and buttered when one day old. Each loaf serves 8.

Lisa Louise Feucht, *Wheat Ridge, Colorado*

HOOSIER HILLS, AUTUMN-HAZE CAKE

¾ cup fresh butter or margarine
1½ cups sorghum molasses
1½ cups very hot water
3 eggs, separated
½ teaspoon vanilla
1½ cups maple sugar
  (brown sugar may be substituted)
4½ cups flour
½ teaspoon salt
1 teaspoon cinnamon
½ teaspoon cloves
3 teaspoons soda
1 cup hickory nut meats, chopped
  (pecans may be substituted)
1 pint whipping cream
  (or prepared whipped topping)

In 3-quart bowl mix butter, sorghum, hot water, egg yolks, vanilla and maple sugar. Beat well. Sift flour, salt, cinnamon, cloves and soda together. Gradually add to butter-egg mixture. Beat egg whites in separate bowl until stiff and fold into batter. Fold in nuts. Bake in 12-by-18-inch pan in 350° oven for 35 to 40 minutes. Cut in squares and serve with whipped cream topping. Serves 24. (May cut recipe in half and bake 20 to 25 minutes in 8-by-10-inch pan.)

Mrs. Leon Pruitt, *Winslow, Indiana*

MOLASSES MARVEL CAKE

1/3 cup butter
1 cup sugar
2 eggs
½ cup molasses
½ teaspoon cinnamon
½ teaspoon nutmeg
¼ teaspoon ginger
3 cups flour
3 teaspoons baking powder
½ teaspoon salt
1½ cups water

Cream butter and sugar. Add eggs, molasses and spices. Sift flour with baking powder and salt. Add alternately with water. Bake in a 9-by-13-inch pan in 350° oven for 30 to 35 minutes. Serves 10 to 12.

Mrs. Franklin C. Ashby, *Smithtown, New York*

"I take it you don't like experiments."

NUTTY, BUTTERMILK CAKE

¾ cup cream style cottage cheese
2 2/3 cups flour
1 teaspoon soda
½ teaspoon baking powder
¼ cup cocoa
¾ teaspoon salt
1 cup granulated sugar
1 cup firmly packed brown sugar
½ cup vegetable shortening
2 unbeaten eggs
1¼ cups buttermilk or
  sour cream
1½ cups walnut meats, chopped

Sieve cottage cheese and set aside. Sift together flour, soda, baking powder, cocoa and salt. Blend granulated sugar and brown sugar with vegetable shortening. Stir in cottage cheese and mix thoroughly. Add eggs, one at a time, and beat well after each addition. Add buttermilk or sour cream, alternately with the dry ingredients, to the creamed mixture, beginning and ending with the dry ingredients. Mix thoroughly after each addition, using low speed on electric mixer. Stir in walnut meats. Turn into well-greased, lightly floured 13-by-9-inch pan. Bake in 350° oven 45 to 50 minutes. Cool and frost with caramel cheese frosting.

Caramel Cheese Frosting

2 cups Kraft caramel sauce
1 (3-ounce) package cream cheese
3 cups confectioners' sugar, sifted
1 teaspoon vanilla

Cream caramel sauce with cream cheese. Gradually add confectioners' sugar, a small amount at a time, until spreadable. Add vanilla and beat until smooth. If too thick, thin with cream.

Diane M. Haley, *Clearwater, Florida*

PINEAPPLE CAKE

2 cups flour
2 cups sugar
2 teaspoons baking soda
2 eggs
1 (#2 can) crushed pineapple
  (and juice)

Mix together flour, sugar and baking soda. Add eggs and pineapple. Pour into greased 9-by-13-inch baking dish and bake at 350° for 40 minutes.

Cream Cheese Frosting

½ box confectioners' powdered sugar
1 stick margarine
1 (8-ounce) package cream cheese
1 teaspoon vanilla

Blend together and pour over hot cake.

Gladys Deems, *Parkersburg, West Virginia*

SOUR CREAM RAISIN DRIZZLE CAKE

5 eggs
¼ cup sugar
1/8 teaspoon salt
½ cup sugar
1 teaspoon vanilla
1½ cups chopped pecans

1½ cups fine vanilla wafer crumbs
1½ teaspoons baking powder
½ teaspoon cinnamon
1 (#2) can raisin-pie mix
½ cup commercial sour cream

Separate eggs, placing whites into large mixing bowl and yolks into smaller mixing bowl. Beat egg whites until foamy; gradually beat in ¼ cup sugar and salt to make a fluffy meringue. Add ½ cup sugar and vanilla to egg yolks. Beat until thick and pale. Pour yolk mixture over meringue; fold together until evenly mixed. Stir together pecans, wafer crumbs, baking powder and cinnamon, and sprinkle over top of meringue mixture. Fold all ingredients together thoroughly. Pour batter into greased 8-inch square baking dish. Bake 35 minutes in 350° oven. While cake is baking, combine raisin-pie mix and sour cream, place on low heat and keep warm until cake is removed from oven. Carefully pour raisin sauce over hot cake. Serve hot or cold. Sprinkle with ¼ teaspoon nutmeg just before serving, if desired. Serves 9.

Caryol Coryell, *Boise, Idaho*

TUTTI-FRUITI LOAF

2 1/3 cups all-purpose sifted flour
2½ teaspoons baking powder
½ teaspoon baking soda
½ teaspoon salt
1/3 cup chopped pitted dates
2/3 cup boiling hot water
2 tablespoons shortening
1/3 cup bananas, mashed

1/3 cup fresh orange juice
1 egg
¾ cup granulated sugar
¼ teaspoon grated orange rind
1/3 cup chopped walnut meats
4 green maraschino cherries, halved
4 red maraschino cherries, halved

Combine first four ingredients and set aside. Pour boiling water over dates in large mixing bowl and add shortening. Set aside to cool. Place mashed bananas in small bowl and cover with orange juice. Beat egg and sugar together. Add dry ingredients alternately with egg mixture to date mixture. Add banana mixture. Fold in orange rind, nut meats and cherry halves. Preheat oven to 325°. Bake 45 to 50 minutes in greased and floured 5-by-9-inch loaf pan.

Mrs. Vivian Jannereth, *Wyoming, Michigan*

VANILLA SURPRISE CAKE

1 butter or yellow cake mix
½ cup sugar
¾ cup margarine, softened
1 cup sour cream

4 eggs, one at a time
1 package instant vanilla pudding
2 teaspoons cinnamon
3 tablespoons brown sugar

Glaze

1 teaspoon vanilla
2 tablespoons milk
1½ cups powdered sugar

Mix cake mix, sugar, margarine, sour cream, eggs and vanilla pudding using a hand mixer or spoon until well blended. In a small bowl mix cinnamon and brown sugar. Grease and lightly flour a bundt cake pan. Spread half of cake mixture in pan. Cover with half of cinnamon mixture. Repeat. Spoon clockwise around pan to distribute cinnamon mixture. Bake at 350° for 1 hour in a preheated oven. Mix vanilla, milk and powdered sugar and glaze cake after it has cooled.

Pamela Warner, *Mission Viejo, California*

VANILLA WAFER CAKE

½ pound butter
2 cups sugar (granulated)
6 eggs
1 (12-ounce) box vanilla wafers

½ cup milk
1 (7-ounce) package flaked coconut
1 cup chopped pecans

Cream butter and sugar. Beat in eggs one at a time, and continue beating until smooth and fluffy. Crush vanilla wafers fine with rolling pin. Add to creamed mixture alternately with milk. Fold in coconut and pecans. Turn into greased and floured tube pan. Bake in 325° oven 1¼ hours or until done. This is a very rich cake, and needs no frosting. It is best made a day before, and will keep fresh many days. Serves 10 to 12.

Patricia Krouse, *Arcadia, California*

LIGHT WHITE CAKE

5 egg whites
3 cups cake flour
3 teaspoons baking powder
1 teaspoon salt

½ cup shortening
2 cups sugar
1 teaspoon vanilla
1 cup milk

Separate eggs and let whites stand while preparing the mixture. Sift dry ingredients together and set aside. Cream shortening and 1 cup of sugar together. Add vanilla and mix well. Add dry ingredients and milk alternately to the mixture, starting and ending with dry ingredients. Beat egg whites slowly, adding remaining 1 cup sugar; beat until stiff. Fold in egg whites. Bake in two 9-inch round cake pans at 350° for 20 to 25 minutes or until an inserted toothpick comes out clean.

Carol D. Hamilton, *Frankfort, Indiana*

STREUSEL TOP PEAR PIE

Cheese Crust:

1 cup flour
½ teaspoon salt
1/3 cup shortening

½ cup grated cheddar cheese
3 to 4 tablespoons water

Sift flour and salt into bowl. Cut in shortening; then mix in the cheese. Sprinkle the water over, 1 tablespoon at a time, and toss gently until mixture holds together. Form into a ball and flatten to ½-inch thickness. Roll out to 1½ inches larger than inverted 9-inch pie pan. Fit in pan, smooth out air bubbles and form high fluted edge.

Filling:

5 cups pears, peeled, sliced
  (about 6 fresh pears)

1 teaspoon grated lemon rind
1 tablespoon lemon juice

Prepare the pears and arrange in layers in pastry-lined pan, sprinkling rind and lemon juice and a dash of cinnamon over each layer.

Streusel Topping:

1 cup flour
½ cup brown sugar
½ cup butter

½ teaspoon cinnamon
¼ teaspoon nutmeg
½ cup chopped nuts

Combine topping ingredients and press over the top of the pears. Bake in preheated 450° oven for 10 minutes, then 35 to 40 minutes at 350° or until the pears are tender. Serves 8.

Ginny Lambert, *Chappaqua, New York*

PAPER PLUM PIE

1 unbaked 9-inch pie shell
4 cups sliced, pitted plums
½ cup sugar
¼ cup flour

¼ teaspoon salt
¼ teaspoon cinnamon
1 tablespoon lemon juice

Topping:

½ cup flour
½ cup sugar
¼ teaspoon cinnamon

¼ teaspoon nutmeg
¼ cup margarine

Quarter the plums and add the sugar, flour, salt, and cinnamon. Mix thoroughly. Sprinkle with the lemon juice. Place in unbaked pie shell. Mix all the topping ingredients together and sprinkle over the pie. Put pie in brown paper bag loosely. Fold over the edges and seal. Set on baking sheet and bake in 425° oven for 1 hour. Let cool in paper bag before removing to serve. Serves 6 to 8.

Mary Anne Berg, *Round Mountain, Nevada*

CHOICE PUMPKIN PIE

1 8-inch pie crust
1 tablespoon butter
1 cup rich milk, scalded
2 large eggs, beaten slightly
2/3 cup white sugar

¼ teaspoon salt
¼ teaspoon ginger
1/3 teaspoon mace
½ teaspoon cinnamon
1 cup light golden pumpkin

Add butter to scalded milk. Mix beaten eggs with sugar. Add salt, ginger, mace and cinnamon to pumpkin and add to egg mixture. Gradually add milk, beating gently just until mixed (not foamy). Pour into unbaked pie crust and bake in preheated 450° oven about 10 to 12 minutes to set crust. Then lower heat to 400° for about 5 minutes. As crust begins to turn a delicate brown on edges, lower heat to about 300° (filling must never start to bubble; if it should, you may have to lower heat to about 275°). Bake until a knife blade inserted in the center of the pie comes out clean. If baked properly, the entire crust should be a light golden brown on the bottom. Serve with butterscotch whipped cream below.

117

Butterscotch Sauce

1¼ cups brown sugar
2/3 cup dark corn syrup
4 tablespoons butter
3/4 cup thin cream

1 pint heavy cream, whipped
1 teaspoon vanilla
1 teaspoon rum flavoring

Mix brown sugar, syrup and butter in pan and bring to a boil, stirring constantly until syrup forms a very soft ball in cold water. Remove from heat and immediately pour in 3/4 cup thin cream. Beat cream into the syrup until thoroughly mixed. Pour into jars, leaving a 2-inch space at the top for mixing the sauce each time before it is served. Cover; refrigerate. This sauce keeps indefinitely under refrigeration. For a double recipe of the pie, whip 1 pint of cream until just stiff. Fold in ½ cup of the butterscotch sauce; add 1 teaspoon vanilla and 1 teaspoon rum flavoring. Serve on top of each slice of pie.

Crust for Pumpkin Pie

3 cups flour
½ teaspoon salt
1 cup lard

1/3 cup vinegar
1/3 cup cold water

Mix flour with salt. Cut in lard until like fine meal. Mix vinegar and cold water and add to flour mixture. Mix until dough will leave the bowl in a clean ball. Wrap in plastic wrap and put in plastic bag. Seal tightly and refrigerate. Makes 2 medium-size double crust pies. Remove from refrigerator an hour or two before using.

Ruth G. Gleason, *Helena, Montana*

FROZEN MINT JULEP PIE

1 1/3 cups crushed zwieback or
    chocolate wafer crumbs
2 tablespoons sugar
¼ cup melted butter
1 envelope unflavored gelatin
½ cup sugar

1/8 teaspoon salt
3 eggs, separated
1 cup light cream
¼ cup bourbon
2 tablespoons mint-flavored jelly
1 cup heavy cream, whipped

Combine crumbs, 2 tablespoons sugar and melted butter. Butter a 10-inch pie plate and press crumbs firmly into the bottom and against sides of pan. Chill.

Combine gelatin, ¼ cup sugar, and salt in medium saucepan. Beat egg yolks lightly and add with light cream and bourbon to gelatin mixture. Cook over low heat, stirring constantly until custard coats the spoon. Stir in mint jelly. Chill until mixture begins to thicken. Beat egg whites to soft peaks. Gradually beat in remaining ¼ cup sugar; beat until meringue is stiff. Fold meringue and whipped cream into the thickened custard. Turn into crumb crust. Place in freezer until firm. To serve: remove to refrigerator shelf 2 hours before cutting. Garnish with sprigs of fresh mint. Makes 8 to 10 servings.

Bess Slagle, *St. Peters, Missouri*

118

SECRET PINEAPPLE CREAM PIE

Crust

1¼ cups all-purpose flour
½ cup toasted coconut
  (Baker's Crunchies)

¼ cup packed brown sugar
½ cup butter or margarine

Filling

1 (8-ounce) package cream cheese
½ cup granulated sugar
2 eggs
¼ cup chocolate-flavored Quik

1 (20-ounce) can crushed
  pineapple, well drained
¼ cup sour cream

To make the crust: Combine flour, coconut, and brown sugar together in a mixing bowl. Cut in butter until crumb mixture forms. Place in ungreased 9-inch pie pan. Bake in 400° oven 12 to 15 minutes, stirring occasionally. Cool and remove 2 tablespoons; set aside. Press the remainder into the pie pan to form a crust.

In a mixing bowl, cream soft cream cheese and sugar together. Beat in two eggs. Remove ½ cup cheese mixture and set this aside. Beat chocolate-flavored Quik into the remaining cheese mixture until well blended and stir in crushed pineapple; place in the prepared crust. In a small bowl, combine the sour cream with the reserved ½ cup cheese mixture. Spoon over the pine-apple layer in the pan. Sprinkle the reserved crumb mixture over the top of pie as desired. Bake in 350° oven for 35 minutes. Cool and chill in the refrigerator before serving. Yield: one 9-inch pie. Serves 8.

Mrs. Gloria Piantek, *Chicago, Illinois*

LUCIE'S PECAN PIE

1 unbaked 10-inch pie shell
2 eggs, beaten
1 cup dark Karo syrup
1 cup white sugar
1 cup milk

1 cup coarsely chopped pecans
  mixed with
2 tablespoons flour
1 teaspoon vanilla
¼ teaspoon salt

Mix all ingredients in order given. Pour into unbaked 10-inch pie shell. Bake 10 minutes at 400°; reduce heat to 350° and continue baking for approximately 40 minutes or until firm in middle. Serves 8.

Lucie E. Moorman, *Fayetteville, North Carolina*

CRANBERRY DREAM PIE

1 baked 9-inch pie shell
24 marshmallows
½ cup milk
2 tablespoons crushed pineapple,
  drained

1 (1-pound) can whole
  cranberry sauce
1 cup chopped pecans
1 cup heavy cream

Melt marshmallows in milk over low heat. Add pineapple, cranberry sauce, and nuts. Whip heavy cream until stiff and fold into cranberry mixture. Pour into baked, cooled pie shell. Chill at least 4 hours before cutting. Serves 6 to 8.

Mrs. Louise Jones, *Harvey, Louisiana*

RAISIN-BLACK WALNUT PIE

1 unbaked 8-inch pie shell
4 eggs, beaten
½ cup brown sugar, packed
½ cup white sugar

¼ cup soft butter or margarine
1½ cups light corn syrup
1 cup black walnuts
1 cup chopped raisins

Combine eggs, sugar, butter and beat until thick and fluffy. Add syrup and beat well. Fold in nutmeats and raisins. Stir gently. Turn into unbaked pie shell and bake in 375° preheated oven for 40 to 50 minutes or until center is firm. Serve plain or topped with ice cream or whipped cream. Serves 6.
Mrs. Lyle H. Camp, *Fullerton, California*

EGGNOG PIE

1 baked 9-inch pastry shell
1½ teaspoons unflavored gelatin
2 tablespoons cold water
3 egg yolks
2/3 cup sugar
1/8 teaspoon salt

1 teaspoon vanilla
2 tablespoons milk
3 egg whites
½ cup heavy cream, whipped
2 to 4 tablespoons rum (optional)
1 teaspoon nutmeg

Soak gelatin in cold water. Beat egg yolks, add 1/3 cup of sugar, salt, vanilla, and milk. Cook over very low heat until thickened. Add gelatin to hot custard mixture. Stir until completely dissolved. Beat egg whites until stiff but not dry; gradually beat in other 1/3 cup of sugar. Fold the custard mixture into the egg whites. Set aside to cool. Fold in whipped cream and rum. Pour into baked pastry shell. Sprinkle top with nutmeg and place in refrigerator until firm. Serves 6 to 8.
Mrs. Frank C. Volpert, *Peru, Indiana*

GRAND FINALE PIE

1 baked 9-inch pastry shell
2 egg whites
1 cup sugar
2 tablespoons water
¼ teaspoon cream of tartar
¼ teaspoon salt

½ cup chocolate chips
1 cup coconut
1 cup chopped nuts
1 teaspoon vanilla
2 cups whipped cream
   or whipped topping

Combine in the top of a double boiler the first five ingredients. Beat with an electric mixer over boiling water for 5 minutes until the mixture stands in stiff peaks. Remove from hot water; add chocolate chips. Let stand about 10 minutes to melt. Fold coconut, nuts and vanilla into the cooked mixture. Cool, then fold in whipped cream. Gently pile into baked pastry shell. Refrigerate for an hour or longer. Serves 6 to 8.
Marleen Carol Johnson, *Robbinsdale, Minnesota*

AFTER DINNER COCKTAIL PIE

Vanilla Wafer Crumb Crust

1½ cups crushed vanilla wafers
1/3 cup melted butter or margarine

Mix vanilla wafer crumbs and melted butter well. Press mixture into bottom and around sides of a 9-inch pie plate. Bake in preheated 375° oven for 8 minutes. Cool.

Cocktail Chiffon Filling

2¾ teaspoons unflavored gelatin
  (little less than 1 package)
¼ cup cold water
¼ cup egg yolks (about 4 large)
5/8 cup sugar
¼ teaspoon salt

1/3 cup fresh lime juice
3 drops green food coloring
1/3 cup light rum
5/8 cup egg whites at room
  temperature (about 4 large)
¼ cup sugar

Soften gelatin in cold water. Beat egg yolks with 5/8 cup sugar and salt until light in top of double boiler. Add lime juice gradually. Cook over boiling water, stirring constantly, until mixture thickens slightly—about 3 to 4 minutes. Do not over cook! Remove from heat. Add softened gelatin and stir in thoroughly. Add food coloring and rum. Chill in refrigerator until mixture thickens—20 to 25 minutes. Beat egg whites until foamy throughout; gradually add remaining ¼ cup sugar and continue to beat until they hold shape in distinct folds. Gently fold the cooled lime-rum mixture into the egg whites. Pour into cooled Vanilla Wafer Crust and chill.

Whipped Cream Topping

1 cup heavy cream
2 tablespoons sugar
½ teaspoon vanilla extract

Combine heavy cream, sugar, and vanilla. Whip until soft peaks form. Spread on pie and decorate with finely grated lime rind.

Donald L. Herman, *Yardley, Pennsylvania*

HELEN'S LEMON PIE

1 baked 8-inch pie shell
1½ cups sugar
3 tablespoons cornstarch
1 tablespoon flour
Pinch of salt

Grated rind and juice of
  1½ lemons
1½ cups water
3 eggs, separated
3 teaspoons sugar

Combine sugar, cornstarch, flour and salt. Add grated lemon rind and juice, water and egg yolks. Cook until thick in double boiler and pour into baked pie shell. Beat egg whites. Gradually add 3 teaspoons sugar and beat until snowy white and stiff. Spread on top of pie. Bake at 350° for 15 minutes to brown. Serves 6.

Mrs. Helen L. Mayo, *Benton, Illinois*

GOLDEN NUGGET DISCOVERY PIE

Pastry:

1¼ cups all-purpose flour
½ teaspoon salt
½ cup shortening

3 tablespoons instant cocoa
3 tablespoons boiling water

Filling:

1/3 cup sugar
1 (8-ounce) package cream cheese
2 tablespoons milk
2 unbeaten eggs

1 tablespoon grated orange rind
1 teaspoon vanilla
½ cup (2 medium) orange sections,
  cut into small pieces

Prepare pastry: Combine the flour and salt. Measure the shortening, instant cocoa and water into mixing bowl; mix well. Add dry ingredients all at once. Stir quickly until mixture holds together. Form into a ball. Flatten to ½-inch thickness. Roll out between lightly floured waxed paper to a circle 1½ inches larger than an inverted 8-inch pie pan. Fit loosely into pan; prick with fork. Fold edge to form rim; flute. Bake at 425° for 12 to 15 minutes.

Prepare orange cheese filling: Cream the sugar and cream cheese with the milk. Add eggs, one at a time, beating well after each. Blend in orange rind and vanilla. Fold in orange sections. Pour into baked shell. Bake at 350° for 20 to 25 minutes, until center is almost firm. Chill. If desired, top with Orange Whipped Cream and sprinkle with chopped toasted almonds about 1 hour before serving. Chill. Serves 6 to 8.

Orange Whipped Cream: Beat 1 cup whipping cream until thick. Stir in 2 tablespoons sugar and 2 tablespoons grated orange rind.

Mrs. Harold Johnston *Anaheim, California*

HARVEY WALLBANGER PIE

22 chocolate wafers rolled fine
4 tablespoons melted butter

Mix wafers and butter together. Pat into a 9-inch greased pie pan covering bottom and sides. Bake 8 minutes. Cool.

22 marshmallows
3/4 cup orange juice
1 tablespoon Cointreau

3 tablespoons Galliano
½ teaspoon grated orange rind
1 pint whipped cream

Melt marshmallows with orange juice in top of double boiler over boiling water. Cool. Add Galliano, Cointreau, and grated orange rind. Refrigerate until slightly thickened. Fold in half of whipped cream. Pour into crust. Refrigerate until firm. Garnish with remaining whipped cream.

Marjorie V. Anderson, *Mount Zion, Illinois*

COOKIES

Just Like Mom's

"Eggs are up. Butter is up."

BUTTERSCOTCH COOKIES

½ cup margarine or butter	baking powder
1½ cups light brown sugar, packed in cup	1 teaspoon soda
	½ teaspoon salt
2 eggs	1 cup sour cream
2½ cups all-purpose flour	1 teaspoon vanilla
½ teaspoon double-action	½ cup nuts (optional)

Cream margarine and sugar. Add eggs and beat. Sift flour, baking powder, soda and salt together and add alternately to batter with the sour cream to which vanilla has been added. Stir in nuts and chill until dough is firm. Drop by teaspoons 2 inches apart on lightly greased baking sheet. Bake 10 to 15 minutes in moderate hot oven (about 400°.)

Brown Butter Icing

1/3 cup butter	1 teaspoon vanilla
1½ cups sifted confectioners' sugar	1 to 2 tablespoons hot water

Melt butter over low heat until golden brown. Blend in confectioners' sugar and vanilla. Stir in slowly 1 to 2 tablespoons hot water until of consistency to spread.

Kathleen Wagner, *Peru, Indiana*

"Would you mind repeating that recipe—without the arsenic?"

BRANDIED CHERRY BUTTER BALLS

Cookie Dough

2/3 cup granulated white sugar
½ teaspoon double-acting
  baking powder
¼ teaspoon salt
½ cup butter or

margarine (softened)
1 large unbeaten egg
1 teaspoon imitation brandy extract
1¾ cups pre-sifted all-purpose flour

Brandied Cherry Filling

30 maraschino cherries
  (drained on paper toweling)
1 tablespoon pure honey

1 teaspoon imitation brandy extract
3 tablespoons walnuts, chopped

Glaze

1 cup unsifted confectioners' sugar
1 tablespoon light corn syrup
2 tablespoons maraschino cherry juice

(heated until hot)
½ teaspoon imitation brandy extract

Prepare brandied cherry filling by placing cherries close together on wax paper. Combine honey and brandy and brush tops of cherries with this combination using a pastry brush. Sprinkle cherries with walnuts. Set aside.

Make cookie dough by combining all ingredients except flour in a large mixing bowl and beat at low speed for 1 minute. Gradually add the flour at low speed until a stiff dough forms (about 1 minute). Form dough into a large ball. Pinch small balls of dough (1 well-rounded teaspoonful) from prepared dough; flatten with fingers in palm of hand to about 1/8-inch thickness. Place 1 brandied cherry with honey and nuts on it in center of dough. Roll to form a ball. Repeat with remaining dough and cherries. Place each ball on an ungreased cookie sheet about 2 inches apart and bake on second and third oven racks from bottom of preheated 350° oven for 12 to 15 minutes, until cookies are delicately golden color.

When cookies are cool, make glaze and spread about ½ teaspoonful on top and sides of each cookie using the inside of teaspoon to spread glaze. Place on wax paper until glaze sets. Yield: 2½ dozen.

Mrs. Gloria Dutrumble, *Uncasville, Connecticut*

HONEY BARS

½ cup shortening
½ cup sugar
½ cup honey
1 egg, well beaten
2/3 cup sifted flour
½ teaspoon baking soda

½ teaspoon baking powder
¼ teaspoon salt
1 cup quick-cooking rolled oats
1 cup flaked coconut
1 teaspoon vanilla
½ cup chopped nuts

Cream shortening, sugar and honey until light and fluffy. Add egg and blend. Sift flour with soda, baking powder and salt; add to creamed mixture. Add oats, coconut, vanilla and nuts. Spread in greased 10½-by-15-inch pan; bake in 350° oven for 20 to 25 minutes. When cool, cut into bars. Yield: 36 bars.

Madelyn E. Jones, *Waterbury, Connecticut*

DROP MOLASSES COOKIES

1 cup brown sugar	1 tablespoon soda
1 cup shortening	4½ cups flour
2 eggs	¼ teaspoon ginger
1 cup molasses (either light or dark)	1 teaspoon cinnamon
1/3 cup hot water	1 teaspoon salt

Cream brown sugar and shortening, add the two eggs and beat well. Blend in the molasses and the 1/3 cup of hot water in which the soda is dissolved. Sift flour with the salt and spices. Mix well all ingredients. Drop by teaspoonfuls on greased and floured pan. Bake at 350° 10 to 12 minutes. Yield: 3 to 4 dozen.

Ruth K. Hunt, *Albion, Michigan*

NUTMEG SUGAR COOKIES

1 cup sugar	1 teaspoon nutmeg
1 cup butter	2 teaspoons baking powder
2 eggs	1 teaspoon vanilla extract
2 cups flour	1 teaspoon orange juice
Pinch of salt	1 tablespoon whiskey

Cream sugar and butter. Add eggs and beat well. Sift together flour, salt, nutmeg and baking powder. Add to batter and mix thoroughly. Add vanilla, orange juice and whiskey. Let stand 4 to 8 hours in refrigerator. Roll out thin and sprinkle with sugar. Cut out and bake 5 minutes in 375° to 400° oven or until light golden. Yield: 100 cookies.

Dorothy Imlay, *St. Joseph, Missouri*

SUPREME OATMEAL COOKIES

1 cup raisins or currants	2 cups flour, sifted
½ cup water	2 cups rolled oats
1 cup shortening	1 teaspoon soda
1 cup white sugar	1 teaspoon salt
2 eggs	

Cook raisins in ½ cup water until tender. Cream together shortening, sugar, eggs. Add dry ingredients and cooked raisins. Drop by teaspoonfuls on greased cookie sheet. Bake at 400° for 8 minutes. Yield: 5 dozen.

Mrs. Earl R. Stevens, *New Bern, North Carolina*

CONGO BARS

2¾ cups flour	2¼ cups light brown sugar
2½ teaspoons baking powder	3 eggs
½ teaspoon salt	1 cup broken nutmeats
2/3 cup vegetable shortening	1 package chocolate chips

Sift flour, baking powder and salt and set aside. Melt shortening. Add sugar and cool slightly. Add eggs one at a time, beating well after each addition. Stir in dry ingredients, nuts and chocolate chips. Bake in 9-by-13-inch pan in 350° oven for 25 to 30 minutes. Cut when almost cool. Yield: 48 bars.

Mrs. Virgil Crockett, *Great Barrington, Massachusetts*

½ cup shortening
1 cup sugar
1 egg
¼ cup evaporated milk or
  light cream
1½ cups flour
¼ teaspoon salt

1 teaspoon baking powder
¼ teaspoon soda
½ teaspoon cinnamon
½ cup cranberry sauce
½ cup chopped nuts
1½ cups Quaker Oats

Cream shortening with sugar; add unbeaten egg and mix well. Then add milk. Sift flour with salt, baking powder, baking soda and cinnamon. Add to first mixture and beat well. Add remaining ingredients. Drop by teaspoonfuls on baking sheet. Bake for 20 minutes at 350°. Yield: 3 dozen.

Mrs. L.O. Kattsoff, *Hyannis, Massachusetts*

RASPBERRY COOKIES

¼ cup butter
1 cup sugar
1 egg
1 (3-ounce) box of
  raspberry gelatin

2 cups flour
½ teaspoon baking soda
½ teaspoon baking powder
½ cup sour milk

Cream the butter and the sugar together. Add egg and gelatin and beat until creamy and smooth. Mix flour, soda and baking powder together and add to batter, along with the milk, a little at a time. Beat until smooth. Drop by teaspoon on greased baking sheet. Bake at 350° for about 15 minutes. Yield: 2 dozen.

Mrs. Irene May, *Fairport, New York*

DIET BUSTER COOKIES

1 cup all-purpose flour
½ teaspoon salt
2 tablespoons orange flavor
  breakfast drink powder
½ teaspoon baking soda
2/3 cup light brown sugar,
  firmly packed
2/3 cup quick-cooking oatmeal

½ stick (2 ounces) butter
½ stick (2 ounces) margarine
1 egg
1 teaspoon vanilla
1 teaspoon water
½ cup seedless raisins
½ cup chocolate morsels

Mix together the first 6 ingredients. Work butter and margarine into mixture as in mixing pie dough. Add egg, vanilla, water, raisins and chocolate morsels. Mix until dough adheres together. Drop by teaspoon on ungreased cookie sheet. Flatten slightly. Bake in 300° oven for 15 minutes, or until delicately browned. Yield: 6 dozen dainty cookies.

Mrs. W. B. Castenholz, Jr., *Norwichtown, Connecticut*

CHOCOLATE SQUARES

2 squares of baking chocolate
1 cup sugar
¼ cup milk
½ teaspoon vanilla

1 tablespoon butter
½ angel or sponge cake,
   cut in 1-inch cubes
Confectioners' sugar

Combine first 5 ingredients in a double boiler, place over water and heat until disolved. Do not boil water. Dip squares of cake in the chocolate mixture; then roll in confectioners' sugar. Let set. The cooled squares may be made ahead of time and stored in a covered container—*not plastic*.
Linda M. Makovitch, *Columbia, South Carolina*

CHRISTMAS CAKE COOKIES

2 pounds dates, chopped
½ pound candied pineapple
½ pound candied cherries
  (red and green)
½ pound shelled almonds
½ pound shelled Brazil nuts
2 ½ cups sifted all-purpose flour

1 teaspoon soda
1 teaspoon salt
1 teaspoon cinnamon
1 cup butter
1½ cups white sugar
2 eggs

Cut fruit into chunks. Blanch almonds and toast until golden. Sift flour, soda, salt and cinnamon. Cream butter, add sugar and mix until smooth. Beat eggs and mix thoroughly into creamed butter and sugar. Add flour mixture, then fruit and nuts. (The mixture is very thick by this time.) Drop by small spoonfuls onto greased cookie sheet. Bake about 10 minutes in 400° preheated oven. *Do not overbake.* Cool slightly before removing from pan. This makes a large quantity of very small cookies. Yield: 5 to 6 dozen medium size.
Mrs. Mariea Creamer, *De Funiak Springs, Florida*

GOLDEN JUBILEE BARS

½ cup butter or margarine
1 cup sugar
1 egg
½ cup apricot nectar juice
2 teaspoons white raisins

2 cups sifted all-purpose flour
½ teaspoon baking powder
½ teaspoon baking soda
2½ cups finely chopped dried apricots

Cream butter and sugar until fluffy. Beat in 1 egg, apricot juice and raisins. Sift flour, baking powder and baking soda. Stir in butter-sugar mixture. Stir in dried apricots. Spread the mixture into a buttered 13-by-9-by-2-inch pan. Bake at 350° for 35 to 40 minutes. Cool in pan.

Jubilee Frosting

½ cup margarine
1 egg
2 tablespoons milk

½ teaspoon apricot nectar juice
3 cups sifted confectioners' sugar

Combine all ingredients. Blend. Beat at medium speed for 2½ minutes. Yield: 30 squares.
Ensign Richard J. O'Brien, *Detroit, Michigan*

DESSERTS

Executive Sweet

"Vanilla? Is that the whitish one with nothing in it?"

CREPES SUZETTE
By George Rector

I suppose that the famous crêpes Suzette are the culminating outburst of what the continent of Europe can do with a pancake. They do call for quite an array of liqueur bottles, but that's not so much of a handicap for the American cook as it was a short time ago, so here goes. Follow my lead and you'll have a stranglehold on one of the most eminent dishes in the world, and one that really deserves its reputation.

You want fairly substantial cakes here, so the eggs take a back seat. The formula for the batter is half a cup of flour, a tablespoon of sugar and a quarter teaspoon of salt, into which go half a cup of milk and one egg, to be stirred coonily until the batter is smooth. Get down the little frying pan—a little more than five inches is the right diameter—butter it well and, when it's hot, pour in just enough batter to cover the bottom when you turn it this way and that. Brown each cake nicely on both sides and stack them in a warm place while you fix the sauce—a process which will fill the kitchen with the odors of paradise, although not the teetotal Mohammedan kind.

Beforehand you've rubbed eight lumps of sugar on the rinds of a lemon and an orange until the sugar is full of the oils—not so difficult as it sounds, although it takes time. Now you can break out the chafing dish that came with the wedding presents and melt a tablespoon of butter in it, adding four lumps of sugar to melt with the butter. Then in go a couple of tablespoons of rum or brandy, ditto of curaçao or Grand Marnier, ditto of benedictine. While that mixture of good things is getting good and hot, you fold four of your pancakes in quarters and then, when the sauce is hot as blazes, drop them in and sort of flop and fiddle with them—toss is the professional word—until they absorb all the sauce. You'll probably be dizzy from the smell, but carry on—repeat the sauce, toss the rest of the pancakes—the above recipe ought to make eight—and then you can sit down and discover what a swell cook you are.

SUITE TOOTH
By Mary Alice Sharpe

To really set the world on fire—or the reverse, which seems to be more what's wanted these days—serve this with hand-cranked honey ice cream.

In a saucepan, mix 1 quart milk, 1 quart heavy cream, 1¾ cups honey. Heat until lukewarm. (Be careful not to scorch.) Chill. Add 1 tablespoon of vanilla. Beat six egg whites until stiff. Using the same beater, beat the egg yolks until thick. Fold into the chilled mixture. Fill chilled freezer container 2/3 full with mixture, adding milk if necessary. Cover tightly, set in freezer tub and follow directions for right amounts of cracked ice and ice cream freezer salt. When mixture is frozen, remove dasher. Pack down ice cream. Replace cover. Return to freezer tub. Set in ice until ready to serve. Makes 1 gallon. To make chocolate, melt 2 cups of chocolate chips in the combination of warm milk and cream.

Since children will eat candy, you might try chocolate-nut squares made by melting a 6-ounce package of semisweet chocolate pieces in 3 tablespoons of honey and 1 teaspoon of vanilla over very low heat; stir just until the chocolate is smooth. Add a cup of coarsely chopped pecans or walnuts and ¼ teaspoon of salt. Pat candy into a buttered pan. When cool, cut into squares.

ALMOND CUSTARD

1 cup almonds, grated or ground
3 eggs
¼ cup sugar
1/8 teaspoon salt
2 cups milk, scalded
1 teaspoon almond flavoring

Sprinkle bottoms of 5 custard cups with half of the almonds and press down. Beat eggs until light. Add sugar and salt. Stir scalded milk into egg mixture. Add almond flavoring and pour into cups. Sprinkle the remaining almonds on top. Bake in 350° oven 40 to 45 minutes. Serves 5.
Mrs. Deveaux M. Ackley, *Jackson, Mississippi*

CRESCENT APPLE DESSERT

1 package refrigerated crescent rolls
4 tablespoons soft butter
1/8 cup cinnamon-sugar mix
2 cups warm applesauce
1½ teaspoons cinnamon
½ cup sour cream
 (or sweet whipped cream)

Open rolls, attach 2 triangles, making a square. Place on cookie sheet. Repeat with other roll. Butter tops and sprinkle with cinnamon-sugar mix. Bake in 350° oven for 10 minutes. Split and butter bottoms. Alternate pastry and applesauce (flavored with cinnamon). End with sugared top. Spread with sour cream or sweet whipped cream. Serve warm. Cut servings with a knife and serve with a spoon. Serves 4.
Mrs. Carl L. Johnson, *Pompton Plains, New Jersey*

APPLE-RAISIN-NUT PUDDING

2 cups chopped tart apples
½ cup raisins
1 cup chopped nut meats,
   preferably pecans
1 cup sugar
¼ cup vegetable shortening
1 egg, large
1 cup flour
1 teaspoon baking powder
1 teaspoon soda
1 teaspoon cinnamon
¼ teaspoon nutmeg
¼ teaspoon salt

Topping

2 tablespoons melted butter
5 tablespoons brown sugar
2 tablespoons cream

Wash, quarter and core unpeeled apples. Run apples through food chopper and measure. Run raisins and nut meats through food chopper. Cream sugar and shortening; add egg and beat until waxy. Sift dry ingredients into creamed mixture; batter will be stiff, the only liquid being the chopped apples. Add chopped apples, raisins and nuts to batter. Beat until well mixed. Pour into 9-by-13-inch shallow pan (greased). Bake about 40 minutes in a 350° oven. Before removing from oven prepare a mixture of butter, sugar and cream and pour over hot cake. Place under broiler until lightly browned. Serve plain or with whipped cream. Serves 12.
Mrs. Artia Chambers, *Skiatook, Oklahoma*

BAVARIAN WONDER BARS

2 eggs, beaten
½ cup vegetable oil
1 cup sugar
16 ounces small-curd creamed
   cottage cheese, sieved
1 teaspoon lemon extract
2 cups all-purpose flour
½ teaspoon salt
3 teaspoons baking powder
2 tablespoons confectioners' sugar

Preheat oven to 350°. Grease and flour 9-inch-square baking pan. Combine first 8 ingredients in bowl. Blend well and stir until smooth, about 72 strokes. Spread in prepared pan and bake at 350° for 55 to 60 minutes, or until toothpick inserted in center comes out clean. Cool in pan 15 minutes and sprinkle with the powdered sugar. Cut into bars and top each with dab of sour cream if desired. Serves 9.

Mrs. Irene Souza, *Sunnyvale, California*

BLUEBERRY PIZZA PREMIER

24 vanilla wafers
¼ cup melted butter
1/3 cup sugar
1 (4-ounce) cup blueberry yogurt
1 (8-ounce) package cream cheese
½ cup sugar
2 eggs
2 tablespoons lemon juice
1 (#2) can blueberry pie filling
1 pint whipped cream

Crush vanilla wafers. Mix with ¼ cup melted butter and 1/3 cup sugar. Place in 8-inch pie or cake tin. Blend yogurt and cream cheese with ½ cup sugar, until smooth. Add eggs. Mix in lemon juice. Pour mixture into pie shell. Bake at 350° for 20 minutes. When cool, pour on blueberry pie filling. Chill thoroughly. Serve with whipped cream. Serves 5 to 6.

Mrs. Claire Garner, *Hillsboro, California*

CHOCOLATE-MINT MERINGUE CLOUD

4 egg whites
¼ teaspoon cream of tartar
1 cup sugar
½ cup finely chopped nuts
1 (4-ounce) package German sweet
chocolate
¼ cup crème de menthe
1 cup heavy cream, whipped to
   soft peaks

Beat egg whites until frothy, add cream of tartar and beat until very stiff. Gradually beat in sugar; fold in nuts all at once. Spread in well-greased 9-inch pie plate, mounding slightly higher on sides. Bake in 275° oven for 20 minutes; increase oven temperature to 300° and bake for 40 minutes longer. (Center *will* sink.) Cool. Melt sweet chocolate over very low heat or in top of double boiler; cool. Blend crème de menthe into cooled chocolate. Fold chocolate mixture and whipped cream together until blended; spoon mixture into cooled meringue shell. Chill until set. Serves 6.

Margaret Blakely, *New Philadelphia, Ohio*

132

COCONUT SOUFFLE

½ cup sugar
2 tablespoons flour
½ cup milk
1 cup coarsely grated fresh
  coconut, packed loosely

Few grains salt
3 egg whites, stiffly beaten
Butter or margarine
Sugar
Hot water

133

Set oven at 300°. Prepare 4 individual molds by buttering and coating inside with sugar. Mix sugar and flour until smooth; gradually stir in milk and bring to boil. Cook 5 minutes over low heat, stirring constantly. Add coconut and salt. When blended, gently fold into the beaten egg whites. Fill molds ¾ full and set in pan of hot water. Bake until set (approximately 15 minutes). Garnish with tinted coconut and serve immediately. These should bake while the main course is being served. Serves 4.

Mrs. Ava Bush, *Grapeland, Texas*

ALOHA CURRIED FRUITS

2 cups canned pineapple chunks,
  drained
2 cups canned pears,
  cut in large pieces
2 cups canned sliced peaches
2 cups canned peeled apricots,
  cut in large pieces

3 bananas, chunked
1 small bottle maraschino cherries,
  uncut
¾ cup firmly packed brown sugar
2/3 cup melted butter
1½ teaspoons curry powder

Drain all cut fruit thoroughly for about 30 minutes. Mix brown sugar, melted butter and curry powder. In a baking dish alternate layers of drained fruit and the curry mixture. Cover and bake in a preheated 350° oven for 1 hour. Good with meats or any meal or served as a dessert. Can be cooked ahead and kept in the refrigerator to use later. Just heat and serve your favorite way. Serves 8 to 10.

Mrs. Buren Rogers, *Fulton, Kentucky*

GINGER-PINEAPPLE CREAM FILLED RING

1 well-beaten egg
1 cup maple syrup
1 cup pineapple yogurt
1 cup soft margarine
2½ cups all-purpose flour

1 teaspoon baking powder
1 teaspoon baking soda
½ teaspoon salt
2 teaspoons ginger

Filling:

1 cup cottage cheese
1 (8¼-ounce) can crushed pineapple

134

Preheat oven to 375°. Butter well a 9-inch tube pan. With mixer on low speed, beat egg, maple syrup, yogurt and soft margarine. Blend well. Combine flour, baking powder, baking soda, salt and ginger. Add half of dry ingredients to egg mixture and stir well. Add remainder of dry ingredients and mix thoroughly. Pour into tube pan and bake 35 to 45 minutes. In blender combine cottage cheese and pineapple and blend until smooth. Use to fill cooled cake which has been sliced in two horizontally. Put top slice back over filling and sprinkle cake with powdered sugar. Serves 8 to 10.

Mrs. Mary Rita Rishe, *Bristol, Rhode Island*

GRAPE-APPLE CRUMBLE

3 cups Concord grapes
1¼ cups granulated sugar
3 tablespoons quick-cooking tapioca
3 tablespoons butter or margarine
1½ tablespoons fresh lemon juice

1/8 teaspoon salt
Red and blue food coloring
1½ cups diced apples (Rhode Island, Greening, Winesap, Cortland or Golden Delicious)

Crumbly Topping

7 tablespoons cold butter
  or margarine
7 tablespoons granulated sugar

¾ cup all-purpose, unbleached flour
6 tablespoons chopped English walnuts

Wash grapes. Separate skins from pulp by squeezing. Put skins aside. Put pulp into saucepan and boil for 5 minutes, stirring. Press through a sieve to remove seeds. To the grape puree add the skins, sugar, tapioca, butter, lemon juice and salt. Cook over moderate heat, stirring, until it thickens. Remove from heat. Add enough food coloring to make a rich purple.

Pare, core and dice apples into ¼-inch cubes. Add to grape mixture. Pour into a buttered 9-inch-round or square baking dish. Cover with crumbly topping and bake in a preheated 375° oven for 18 to 20 minutes. Serve at room temperature. To prepare topping: Cut cold butter, sugar and flour together with a pastry blender as for pie crust. Thoroughly mix in the walnuts. Squeeze dough together to form small lumps. Sprinkle over grape-apple mixture in baking dish.

Mrs. W. Edward Frank, *Abington, Pennsylvania*

HAWAIIAN SOUFFLE

3 tablespoons butter
4 tablespoons flour
1 cup milk
4 tablespoons sugar

1/8 teaspoon salt
1 cup crushed pineapple, drained
4 egg yolks
5 egg whites

Butter soufflé dish (1½-quart) and sprinkle with 1 tablespoon sugar. Melt butter in saucepan; stir in flour. Gradually add milk and sugar, stirring until smooth. Cook until sauce is thick. Add salt, pineapple and stir well. Beat egg yolks until lemon-colored; add gradually to mixture, stirring constantly. Cool. This portion may be made in advance.

Just before baking, beat egg whites until stiff enough to hold a rounded peak. With spatula thoroughly fold 2/3 of beaten egg whites into sauce. Now add remaining whites and fold in very gently. Pour into soufflé dish and bake in preheated oven at 350° for 45 minutes. Chill.

Put into dessert dishes, top with whipped cream. Sprinkle with coconut. Top with a cherry or strawberry. Serves 6.

Carol M. Johnson, *Glenwood Springs, Colorado*

REGAL LEMON DELIGHT

1 (7¼-ounce) package vanilla wafers
½ teaspoon salt
2 cups sugar (reserve ½ cup
  for egg whites)
½ cup cornstarch
4 eggs, separated

1¾ cups water
½ cup lemon juice
8 ounces cream cheese
4 tablespoons grated lemon rind
1 cup whipping cream, whipped

Crush wafers and use 2/3 of the crumbs to line a 9-by-12-by-2-inch baking dish. Reserve remaining crumbs for topping. Prepare lemon filling as follows: In a heavy kettle combine salt, 1½ cups sugar, cornstarch and 4 egg yolks. Blend and add water with lemon juice. Cook over medium heat until thick, stirring constantly. Add cream cheese and lemon rind. Blend well and cool. In a separate bowl, beat egg whites until stiff, gradually adding ½ cup sugar. Fold into lemon mixture. Pour into crumb shell. Whip cream and spread over lemon mixture. Sprinkle crumbs over top and chill overnight. Serves 16.

Marian Lundquist, *San Diego, California*

SUNNISIGH
SMACKAROON SQUARES

1 (8-ounce) can refrigerated
  quick crescent dinner rolls
1 cup (12-ounce jar) caramel
  ice cream topping
1 egg, beaten
1 1/3 cups (3½-ounce can)

angel flake coconut
1 (2-ounce) envelope whipped
  topping mix, used dry
½ teaspoon vanilla
¼ teaspoon almond extract
1 tablespoon butter, melted

Separate crescent dough into 2 large rectangles. Press rectangles into an ungreased 13-by-9-inch baking pan. In medium bowl, combine remaining ingredients. Spread evenly over dough. Bake at 375° for 15 to 20 minutes until crust is golden brown. Cool slightly; cut into squares and serve warm or cold with whipped cream or ice cream. Yield: 24 bars.

Thomas O. Davis, *Waynesboro, Mississippi*

INSTANT MOCHA CREAM LOG

1 cup heavy cream
1 cup cold milk
2 teaspoons instant coffee
1 (4½-ounce) package instant

chocolate pudding
1 cup chopped nuts
1 (6-inch) bakery jelly roll

Pour cream and milk into a deep mixing bowl. Add instant coffee and pudding. Beat until well mixed, about 1 minute. Fold in nuts. Gently unroll jelly roll and spread with half of pudding mixture. Roll up and frost with remaining pudding mixture. Freeze until firm. Slice into 6 servings.
Mrs. Olga Jason, *New Bedford*, *Massachusetts*

ELEGANT MAI TAI MOUSSE

18 ladyfingers, split
2 envelopes unflavored gelatin
½ cup pineapple juice
   (from crushed drained pineapple)
5 egg yolks
¾ cup sugar
¼ teaspoon salt
1 cup milk, scalded
1/3 cup lime juice

1/3 cup white rum
1 (#211) can crushed pineapple,
   well drained
5 egg whites
½ cup sugar
1 cup heavy cream, whipped
¼ cup chopped macadamia nuts
   or walnuts

Line sides and bottom of 9-inch spring pan with split ladyfingers. Soften gelatin in pineapple juice. Beat egg yolks in top of double boiler. Stir in sugar and salt. Blend in milk, cook over boiling water, stirring for 5 minutes or until thickened. Blend in gelatin-pineapple mixture, lime juice and rum. Add well-drained pineapple. Chill until thickened but not set. Beat egg whites, adding sugar. Fold pineapple custard and whipped cream into egg whites. Pour into lined pan. Chill several hours or overnight. To serve, remove pan rim. Sprinkle with nuts. Serves 12.

ORANGE BABA DESSERT

1 (13¾-ounce) package hot roll mix
¾ cup warm water
2 eggs
2 tablespoons melted butter

2 tablespoons sugar
1½ teaspoons grated orange rind
1 tablespoon brandy (or
   2 teaspoons vanilla)

In large mixing bowl, combine warm water with yeast (from hot roll mix). Stir until dissolved. Stir in eggs, melted butter, sugar, orange rind, and brandy. Add flour a little at a time and beat well, until batter resembles cake batter. Butter a 9-inch torte pan; half fill, spooning into pan. Cover and let rise until double in size (about 30 to 45 minutes). Preheat oven to 375°. Bake 20 to 30 minutes, or until brown. (If browning too fast, cover with brown paper.) Turn baba out on a serving dish and baste with hot syrup until all syrup is absorbed. Garnish with sliced almonds. Serves 6.

Orange Baba Syrup

Bring to a boil 1 cup sugar and 1 cup water. Add 1 tablespoon butter and one 6-ounce can frozen orange juice concentrate.
Mrs. Joe Hrvatin, *Spokane*, *Washington*

SWEDISH HARVEST PUDDING

¼ cup fine graham cracker crumbs
1 (16-ounce) can pumpkin pie
 filling (seasoned and sweetened,
 not plain canned pumpkin)
2 cups small-curd
 creamed cottage cheese

¼ cup liquid honey
1 large egg, lightly beaten
1 teaspoon ground cardamom
½ cup chopped walnuts
½ cup seedless raisins

Preheat oven to 450°. Grease a 1½-quart baking dish, dust with graham cracker crumbs. Blend all remaining ingredients and pour into baking dish. Bake 10 minutes at 450°; then reduce heat to 325° and bake another 40 to 50 minutes or until knife inserted near center comes out clean. May be served warm or cool, with pour-cream or a custard sauce. Serves 6.

Mrs. Selma Albrecht, *Minneapolis, Minnesota*

SWEDISH PUDDING

1 envelope unflavored gelatin
½ cup cold water
5 eggs, separated

1 cup white sugar
Juice and grated rind of 1 lemon
1/8 teaspoon salt

Dissolve the gelatin in water in a double boiler for 5 minutes. Cool to lukewarm. Use a large mixing bowl to beat the egg yolks. Add the sugar a little at a time. Mix well. Add the lemon juice and rind. Continue beating. The more you beat the lighter in color will be the mixture. Add the cooled gelatin mixture and beat more. Beat the whites and add the salt. The egg whites must be stiff. Fold into the egg mixture. Pour into a fruit compote and chill until firm.

Suggestion: Make this dessert in the evening and let stand overnight. Serve it with whipped cream and line the bowl with maraschino cherries. Sprinkle with toasted almonds as a garnish. This is a very attractive dessert and good after a heavy dinner. Serves 6 to 8.

Andrew Wilson, *Lakeland, Minnesota*

MRS. PLUMB'S PUDDING

1 cup sifted flour
1¼ teaspoons baking powder
½ teaspoon baking soda
1 teaspoon cinnamon
1 teaspoon ground cornflakes
1 teaspoon anise powder

½ cup suet, shredded
 (or vegetable shortening)
½ cup sugar
¾ cup dried fruit
 (raisins, apricots and dates)
½ cup milk

Grease 1½-quart mold. Sift flour with baking powder, soda, cornflakes and spices. Stir in suet, sugar and dried fruit. Mix together with enough milk to make a soft consistency. Pour mixture gently into a 1½-quart mold. Cover top with kitchen foil and steam for 3 hours or until well raised. Serve with whipped cream.

To Steam:
Place mold on rack in a deep kettle. Fill the kettle with enough water to come halfway up the sides of the mold. Make sure the water boils steadily, but not vigorously, while steaming. When done, remove mold from kettle. Cool 10 minutes and unmold pudding. Serves 6.

Mrs. Hank O'Brien, *Detroit, Michigan*

TROPICAL TORTE

Cake:

2¼ cups flour
1½ cups sugar
1 teaspoon salt
2 teaspoons baking powder
¼ teaspoon soda
½ cup vegetable shortening

1 cup mashed bananas
¼ cup milk
1 teaspoon vinegar
1 teaspoon vanilla
2 eggs
1 cup finely chopped pecans

Filling:

1½ cups sugar
2 tablespoons flour
2 eggs, beaten

1 stick butter
1 cup drained crushed pineapple
1½ cups coconut

Cake: Sift flour, sugar, salt, baking powder and soda into large mixing bowl. Add shortening, bananas, milk, vinegar, vanilla and eggs. Beat 3 minutes. Grease and sprinkle with pecans two 9-inch cake pans. Pour in batter and bake 30 minutes at 350°. Cool and split layers crosswise. Alternate layers of cake and filling, ending with filling on top.
Filling: Cook sugar, flour, eggs, butter and pineapple until thick. Add coconut. Cool. Serves 8 generously.
Mrs. J.R. Hickman, *St. Petersburg, Florida*

WALNUT MERINGUE DREAM

4 egg whites (at room
   temperature and a few days old)
Pinch of salt
1½ cups of superfine white sugar

1½ teaspoons vinegar
1½ teaspoons vanilla
1 cup ground walnuts
1 cup heavy cream, whipped

Oil and flour (or spray with Pam) an 8-inch springform tin and preheat oven to slow (300°). Beat egg whites with the salt at full speed until they stand in peaks. Sift sugar and gradually sprinkle in 1 tablespoon at a time, beating at high speed only until all sugar has been thoroughly mixed in. Then gently fold in vinegar, vanilla and walnuts. Put into the prepared tin and cook in the slow oven for 1 hour. Turn the heat off completely and leave the meringue in the oven until cold. When the meringue is cold remove from tin. The top may crumble slightly; if not, gently tap with knife handle until it crumbles just a little. Just before serving, pile whipped cream (unsweetened) on top of meringue. Then over this lightly dribble some chocolate syrup and sprinkle with some chopped walnuts. Serves 6.
Mrs. Penni Dean, *Chicago, Illinois*

INTERNATIONAL SPECIALTIES

The World in Your Hand

"A little more wine, my duck?"

BALLOTINE DE DINDE
By Ruth M. Malone

One of the world's experts on bringing exciting new ideas to family dining is Ruth M. Malone, author of The Dogpatch Cook Book, Where to Eat in the Ozarks, *the* Holiday Inn International Cook Book, *and articles beyond mention for national magazines, among them* The Saturday Evening Post. *It is from her recipes in the* Post, *specializing in international flavor, that the following are selected. The peripatetic lady really knows whereof she speaks, worldwide.*

10- to 12-pound turkey
3 black truffles
   (1 small can)
½ cup shelled and
   skinned pistachio
   nuts
6-ounce piece of
   cooked ham
6-ounce piece of
   cooked smoked
   tongue
¾ pound veal and ¾
   pound pork ground
   together very finely
3 eggs
½ teaspoon ground
   thyme
Pinch of allspice
2 teaspoons salt
Dash of pepper
1 clove garlic
1 cup dry port
   wine or cognac
2 onions, chopped
Pepper and salt
½ pound butter
Needle, white
   thread
Butcher's twine

The day before: put out all your ingredients. Dice the truffles, shell pistachio nuts, cut ham and tongue into finger-shaped pieces. Put pork and veal mixture into a large mixing bowl. Add lightly beaten eggs, thyme, allspice, salt, pepper, crushed clove of garlic, ¾ cup of port or cognac. Mix till light. Gently sauté the onion in a quarter pound of butter. Take almost 10 minutes to do this, cooking onions so gently that they only yellow and do not brown. Add onions and butter to the bowl. Mix thoroughly. This is the stuffing. Put boned turkey flat on the table, skin side down. Season the meat side (inside) with pepper and remaining wine. Spread a layer of stuffing inside the turkey. Then sprinkle pistachio nuts, truffles, ham and tongue over it. Repeat both steps twice. Sew up turkey. Tie in 4 places as you would a rolled roast, making sure stuffing does not go to the ends. Salt, pepper and brush the skin with melted butter. Store in refrigerator until four hours before dinner. Christmas Day: Roast turkey breast side up in a 350-degree oven, allowing 20 minutes per pound. Keep basting top and sides to insure even browning. Serve with natural pan gravy. Serves 8 to 10 easily. If you wish to serve a wine with the dinner, Chassagne Montrachet 1959 is recommended. It is a mildly sweet white wine that will suit most palates.
(Note: The pâté maison used for stuffing the ballotine makes a delicious stuffing for a turkey that has all its bones.)

MERINGUE GLACEE

A memorable dessert that is light enough to follow a Christmas dinner is suggested. You may also use peach ice cream and peach slices, or other combinations.

4 egg whites
Pinch of salt
¼ teaspoon cream
  of tartar
1 cup sifted
  granulated sugar

1 teaspoon almond extract
1 quart strawberries
1 cup red
  currant jelly
2 tablespoons cognac
1 quart ice cream

Cover cookie sheet with greased, unglazed brown paper. Beat egg whites until foamy. Add salt and cream of tartar and continue beating until peaks form. Add sugar very slowly, beating until sugar is dissolved. Add almond extract. Drop by mounded teaspoonful onto brown paper. Bake in 250-degree oven for 1½ hours. At the end of the time, turn off oven, open door and allow meringues to cool in the oven. Leave on paper until ready to use. Christmas Day: Hull the strawberries. Melt the currant jelly and cognac over a low fire. Put ice cream on the dish, surround it with strawberries. Pour warm sauce on the berries and top with meringues.

RED SNAPPER A LA VERACRUZANA
(Huachinango a la Veracruzana)

1 2½-pound red snapper
2½ cups chopped tomatoes
2 onions, chopped
3 green peppers, chopped
3 cloves garlic, crushed
1 bunch parsley,
  chopped fine
2 chili peppers,
  chopped fine
  (small elongated
  green chili)

1/3 cup finely chopped
  green olives
1/3 cup capers
4 tablespoons vinegar
8 jalapeño peppers
  (cut in half,
  fried and cut in strips)
1 pint oil
1 teaspoon oregano
Salt and pepper
¼ pint dry sherry

Cut red snapper into 6-ounce fillets. Saute the tomatoes in a skillet, adding onions, then green peppers, garlic, parsley and chili peppers. Then add chopped olives, capers, vinegar and jalapeño strips. Blend in oil. Season with oregano, salt and pepper. Simmer slowly until all is tender and thickened. Add sherry during last part of cooking.

In a separate skillet, heat a little oil and add well-washed red snapper fillets. Cover fish with sauce. Cover and cook over low heat 20 minutes. Keep fish from sticking with wide spatula. Serve with rice. Serves 4 to 6.

AUNT ELIZA'S BID FOR FAME
By Sophie Kerr

In my Scotch-Irish family there was one aunt who married among the Pennsylvania Dutch, and it was she who, ever-blessed, imparted the recipe for making the local form of peach pie. It is as follows: Line a pie pan with the raw crust and fill it with halves of very ripe yellow peaches, hollow side up. Lay the peaches close together, sprinkle heavily with granulated sugar, then pour in enough thick sour cream to cover the peach halves, and sprinkle on more sugar if needed. Then put on your crisscross strips, pinch them well at the edges, and slide this concoction info the oven for a slow, careful baking. If you want to add two or three kernels taken from cracked peach stones, you'll have a subtle bitter-almond flavor—indeed, a few peach kernels add chic to any peach pie, whether made a la Aunt Eliza or not.

IRELAND'S GIFT TO APPETITES
By George Rector

If it's a short-term trip, you can get the ingredients ready before you start, and pack them in a large pot and two saucepans. You'll want to scrape six medium-sized carrots, peel four potatoes, dice two green peppers into inch cubes, cut up half a cup of leeks and half a cup of celery crosswise, lay in a dozen small white onions and a cup of canned tomato pulp. Also you pack along a mixture of a teaspoon of mixed mustard, and a tablespoon each of Worcestershire sauce, A-1 sauce and tomato ketchup. That begins to sound good already to me. Also—this is the business end—three pounds chuck of lamb, a pound of breast of lamb and a pound chuck of beef, all cut into two-inch cubes and with as much fat as possible trimmed off the lamb. It sounds like food for a regiment, I know, but don't try to get more than six grown people into one stew if you serve it outdoors after waiting for it to cook.

Simmer your beef for an hour. Then start the lamb in a separate pan and simmer both for another half hour, skimming the fat off the lamb water all the time. Then lamb and beef go into the big pot, along with the liquid, plus the potatoes and carrots quartered, the green peppers, the onions, leeks and celery. Let them all coop up harmoniously for half an hour. Ten minutes before that, put in the tomato pulp and the seasoning, and take the pot off the fire—but keep it right next door, so she'll stay plenty hot. At Dinty Moore's they garnish the end product with a sprinkling of peas and a tablespoon of chopped parsley, but it's a roaring, ranting fine dish without that extra wrinkle and well worth the two hours of nursing it calls for. Let the rest of the party go off and chase butterflies or listen to the echo; you stick around and startle your and their palates with this stew of stews.

JEWISH COOKING
By Sylvia Schur

"Eat a little something," that familiar, age-old Jewish welcome, is an almost unnecessary invitation. In the presence of good Jewish cooking, it is nearly impossible to stop eating. "And it isn't just the food itself," explains one young matron. "It's partly the mood and the memories. I remember that as a child in our New York neighborhood, with the aromas of gefilte fish, roast chicken and yeast cake coming from every house, I couldn't get home fast enough. It was the same every Friday. And the baking of challah, *that wonderful Sabbath bread, has as much religious fervor as cooking skill. Even now such smells seem to me like Peace and Love and Warmth. You know what I mean. If Betty Crocker could put those smells up in box mixes, we could end juvenile delinquency."*

Jewish cooking today is an amalgam of contributions, picked up by generations of merchants and migrants who wandered the countries of the earth. In the melting-pot processes of the big city these culinary contributions have simmered down to a tasty heritage known as "New York-style Jewish cooking." In the more than three centuries since the first Jewish pioneer group arrived in New Amsterdam, this influence has spread till most cities in the United States today can enjoy its specialties.

GEFILTE FISH

3 pounds carp	2 eggs
2 pounds whitefish	¼ cup water
1 pound yellow pike	Salt, white pepper
3 onions	1 tablespoon cracker meal
Salt, whole peppercorns	2 carrots, scraped

Have fish dealer fillet fish, reserving heads and bones for stock. Salt fillets and refrigerate. Cover heads, bones, two peeled onions, salt and peppercorns with 1 quart water; bring to boil, simmer 20 minutes. Meanwhile put fish fillets and 1 onion through grinder with fine blade. Place in wooden chopping bowl. Add eggs, lightly beaten with water, salt, pepper and cracker meal. Chop mixture till light and well blended. Moisten hands with cold water and shape into loose balls. Slip into boiling stock with a spoon, add water if necessary to cover and simmer 1½ hours. Add carrots and cook another half hour until fish balls are white and about twice original size. Lift fish balls out with slotted spoon. Remove carrots, slice and set aside. Strain stock and pour half over fish. Pour remainder into jar; refrigerate to set. Serve cold, garnishing the fish with sliced carrot and chilled stock. Serves about 12.

SWEET AND SOUR POT ROAST

6 pounds beef
2 large onions, sliced
1 clove minced garlic
¾ cup of water or stock
2 bay leaves
2 tablespoons lemon juice

or vinegar
1 tablespoon brown
 sugar
3 tablespoons ketchup
½ cup raisins
Salt

Brown meat in hot fat on all sides, using heavy pot. Add onions and garlic, cook till brown. Add water or stock and bay leaves; cover and simmer one hour. Add lemon juice and brown sugar. Cover and simmer another hour. Add ketchup, raisins and salt. Cover and cook ½ hour. Serve hot with potato pancakes, noodles or brown rice. Serves 6 to 8 persons.

NOODLE FRUIT CAPON STUFFING

½ pound broad noodles, cooked
4 tablespoons fat (preferably
 chicken fat)
1 medium onion, minced
Liver and gizzards, chopped
1 tablespoon salt
1 teaspoon paprika

¼ teaspoon pepper
¼ teaspoon ginger
2 tablespoons minced parsley
1 cup minced apples
1 cup prunes, stewed and cut
Grated rind of 1 orange
1 beaten egg

Cook noodles, drain, rinse with cold water and drain well. Toss with one tablespoon of fat. Heat remaining fat, add onions, liver, gizzards, seasonings and parsley; brown. Stir in apples, prunes and grated rind. Add mixture to noodles in a large bowl, toss. Stir in beaten egg. Pack stuffing loosely in cavity of 6- to 8-pound capon, truss. Rub outside of capon with oil, place breast up in shallow roasting pan and bake in 350° oven for two to two and a half hours, basting with oil from time to time.

SABBATH CHOLENT

3 to 4 pounds of beef
1 pound dried Lima beans
3 large onions, sliced
¼ cup chicken fat
Salt, pepper and paprika

1 small clove garlic
½ pound barley
2 tablespoons flour
Boiling water to cover

For the meat use flanken or brisket. Soak beans overnight; then drain. Using heavy-duty pot, brown onions in hot fat, remove. Rub meat generously with salt, pepper, paprika, and garlic. Brown well in hot fat. Add all ingredients; sprinkle lightly with flour. Add boiling water to cover. Cover tightly and bring to boil. Taste, adjust salt, pepper. To finish cooking, place covered pot in 250° oven overnight and until noon next day or cook in 350° oven for 3 to 4 hours. Serves 10 to 12.

RICH NOODLE PUDDING

½ pound medium egg noodles
3 tablespoons butter
1 package (8 ounces) cream cheese
½ pound cottage cheese
½ cup sour cream
3 eggs, separated
½ teaspoon salt

½ cup sugar
1 teaspoon cinnamon
1 cup sliced peeled apples
¼ cup broken walnut meats
1 teaspoon grated lemon rind
½ cup white raisins

Cook noodles in boiling, salted water. Drain. Toss with butter in large bowl. Break up cream cheese with fork, add cottage cheese and sour cream and beat until light. Add egg yolks, beat well. Pour over noodles in bowl. Add remaining ingredients, except egg whites, and mix well. Beat egg whites stiff, fold in. Pour into greased casserole. Bake in 350° oven about 45 minutes, or until browned. Serves 6.

DANISH-AMERICAN WINNER
By Robert W. Wells

Mrs. Beck's Honskekod suppe *(chicken soup) with meatballs and dumplings:*

Soup:

One 3- to 4-pound chicken
2 teaspoons salt
1 soup wisp (celery leaves and

parsley tied together)
1 small onion
2 or 3 small whole carrots

Meatballs:

1 pound ground pork
1 cup milk
1 medium-sized onion
1/3 cup flour (or bread

crumbs)
1 egg
1 teaspoon salt
½ teaspoon pepper

Dumplings:

1 cup boiling water
½ cup butter
1 cup flour

4 eggs
½ teaspoon salt

Cut up chicken. Place in boiling water. Add wisp, onion, carrots, salt. Water should just cover chicken. Simmer until done.

To make meatballs, stir milk into ground pork, adding grated onion, flour or bread crumbs, egg, salt, pepper. Mix thoroughly. Form into balls. Boil until done in salt water.

Dumplings: Melt butter in boiling water. Add flour and beat until smooth. Cool, then add eggs, one at a time, and beat well. Add salt. Use teaspoon to drop dumpling mix into hot but not boiling salt water. Bring to boil, agitating water gently so dumplings will turn over. Boil about two minutes.

Put several dumplings and meat balls into each dish. Slice carrots and put a few slices into each dish. Remove chicken from soup and serve it separately. Remove wisp, which may be thrown away or eaten by the cook. Pour soup on top of dumplings and meatballs. Garnish with sprinkled parsley. Serves 6 to 8.

VONDERFUL NICE
By Bill Wolf

Picnics bring out the cat in Dutch women. They contrive to sample rival cooks' products, conceal their own recipes and try to acquire those of other women. A confirmed taster will try everything on the long tables, then say to a select group of friends: "That potato salad made by Sadie Habecker, it's vonderful nice, of course, but"—she will pause judiciously—"it don't seem to have zaktly the right amount of bacon drippin's. Do you spose she uses celery salt as vell as celery?"

Everything really did taste "vonderful nice"—Dutch cold pressed chicken, cold ham, beef, pork, cold fried chicken, pickled and deviled eggs, an amazing variety of cakes and pies, and always the Dutch potato salad. There are many variations. This is the way I know it best:

Boil and cube eight potatoes or cut them in thick half slices. Add diced celery, four chopped hard-boiled eggs, at least one onion chopped fine—even more skilled cooks scrape the juice from the onion over the potatoes. Now for the dressing: Fry eight slices of bacon cut into small pieces. In a separate bowl, mix a half cup of water, same amount of vinegar, a half teaspoon of salt, quarter teaspoon each of dry mustard and black pepper, two well-beaten eggs. Stir and add to hot bacon and fat.

After this mixture thickened on the stove, it was poured over the cold ingredients, everything was stirred slightly and set aside to cool. A somewhat similar sour dressing, minus the mustard and plus some butter, cream and sugar, is poured hot over dandelions in the spring for greens, or on lettuce leaves.

SHOOFLY PIE

Then there are the pies, such as the famous shoofly, which are really cakes in a pastry shell. Addicts of the shoofly—the name is probably a corruption of chouflour, *since the finished pie somewhat resembles a cauliflower—are sharply divided into Wets and Drys, although both camps would probably agree that the molasses that goes into a shoofly is the most important factor. With many perfectionist cooks, the bottled variety will not do; real barrel molasses is a necessity. In any case, ¾ cup of baking molasses is mixed with a well-beaten egg yolk and ¾ cup of boiling water in which 2 teaspoons of baking soda have been dissolved. In another bowl, ¾ cup of flour is sifted with ½ cup of brown sugar; 1/8 teaspoon each of nutmeg, ginger and cloves; ½ teaspoon of cinnamon and ¼ teaspoon of salt, and worked into 2 table-spoons of shortening to form crumbs. A pie dish is lined with pastry, and alternate layers of the liquid and the crumb mixture are added, topping with the latter. It is baked at 450° until the edges are brown, then the oven is reduced to 350°, and the shoofly is baked until firm. For a "wetter" shoofly—one with a stickier bottom—more molasses is added.*

Also characteristically Pennsylvania Dutch are milk pies. As the name implies, milk or buttermilk is poured into a crust, a bit of sugar and butter are added with 2 teaspoonfuls of flour and a dash of cinnamon and nutmeg, and the whole baked in a hot oven. All laws of cookery would indicate that the only result would be an inedible mess and an oven in need of immediate cleaning, but strangely enough a delicate custard emerges.

SPREBUGIUN
(Italian Vegetables)

2 pounds potatoes
½ pound green beans
1 large white onion
¾ pound zucchini, sliced
¾ pound curly cabbage,
   cut in chunks

1 small onion, finely chopped
2 large cloves garlic, minced
1 cubed salt pork
¾ cup Parmesan cheese
½ cup crumbled crisp bacon

Peel potatoes and cut into large chunks. Remove all strings from beans. Quarter the onion. Cook the potatoes, beans and onions in boiling salted water for 15 minutes. Add zucchini and cabbage and cook until tender. Sauté finely chopped onion and minced garlic in salt pork until golden. When vegetables are done, drain in colander until very dry. Place in heated bowl along with the hot pork and onion mixture. Season with salt. Add Parmesan cheese and mash thoroughly before serving. Sprinkle with more grated cheese and crumbled bacon.

Angela de Nevi, *Reno, Nevada*

GHIVETCH
(Mexican Vegetables)

1 cup thinly sliced carrots
1 cup snap beans, cut
   diagonally into ½-inch slices
1 cup diced potatoes
½ cup celery, cut
   into ¼-inch slices
2 medium tomatoes,
   cut into quarters
1 yellow squash, thinly sliced
1 zucchini, thinly sliced
½ onion, thinly sliced
½ head cauliflower,
   cut into flowerets

¼ cup thin strips
   sweet red pepper
½ cup green peas
1 cup vegetable broth
   or beef bouillon
1/3 cup olive oil
3 cloves garlic, chopped
2 teaspoons salt, approximately
½ bay leaf
½ teaspoon savory
½ teaspoon tarragon
Grated Parmesan cheese
Jack cheese, cut in thin slices

Combine all vegetables in a shallow baking dish. Heat broth and add oil, garlic, salt, bay leaf, savory, tarragon. (Crush fine the dried herbs.) Bring broth mixture to a boil, pour over vegetables and cover casserole with tight-fitting lid. Bake at 350° 1 hour. Gently mix vegetables twice during cooking. At the end of cooking time, uncover casserole, sprinkle generously with Parmesan cheese and cover completely with sliced Jack cheese. Place under broiler until cheese is melted and bubbly. Serves 4 to 6.

Mrs. Oral Sidenfaden, *Pauma Valley, California*

AUTHENTIC SPANISH BEAN SOUP

¾ pound garbanzos (chick-peas)
1 teaspoon salt
  (for soaking garbanzos)
1 beef bone
1 ham bone
1½ quarts water

4 ounces whole bacon
1 onion
½ pound potatoes
1 pinch saffron
1 tablespoon salt
1 chorizo (Spanish sausage)

Soak garbanzos overnight with one teaspoon salt in water to cover. Before cooking, drain salted water and put garbanzos, beef bone and ham bone in 1½ quarts water. Cook 45 minutes over slow fire. Fry bacon and finely chopped onion. Place in pan, adding potatoes, saffron and salt. When potatoes are almost done, add chorizo cut in thin slices. Simmer 20 to 25 minutes. Serves 6.

Shirley Martin, *Tampa, Florida*

LATVIAN MIDSUMMER CHEESE

½ gallon fresh milk
5 pounds dry cottage cheese
1 stick butter or margarine

4 eggs
1 teaspoon salt
2 tablespoons caraway seeds

In a large kettle pour milk. Add dry cottage cheese and stir until it begins to boil. Turn off heat. Place cheesecloth in a large bowl. Add the boiled mixture. Take the corners of the cheesecloth to the top, let the liquid drip out, then squeeze cheesecloth as dry as possible. Place dry cheese in a bowl with the butter or margarine, eggs, salt and caraway seeds. With wooden spoon stir until it is well mixed and the cheese is solid in one piece.

Irma Henkels, *Indianapolis, Indiana*

SERINA KAKER
(Norwegian Cookie)

1¾ sticks butter or margarine
1 1/8 cups sugar
2 eggs, separated
2¼ cups flour, sifted

1½ teaspoons baking powder
1 teaspoon vanilla
50 almonds, chopped

Cream butter and sugar. Add 2 egg yolks and one egg white and mix well. Sift flour and baking powder together and add to batter. Add vanilla and form small round balls about one inch in diameter. Place on lightly greased cookie sheet and press down with bottom of glass. Brush with other egg white and sprinkle with almonds. Bake in 350° oven until very light golden. Do not let brown. Yield: 4 dozen.

Mrs. William Wesely, *Wayne, New Jersey*

HUNGARIAN KALACS

2 fresh yeast cakes
1 cup lukewarm water
4 tablespoons sugar
½ cup butter, melted

4½ cups flour
2 egg yolks
1 teaspoon salt

Filling:

½ cup milk
1½ pounds ground walnuts
½ cup sugar

1 tablespoon butter
1 teaspoon lemon juice

Crumble yeast and add water and sugar. Let stand 5 minutes. Mix melted butter and flour as for pie crust. Make a well and add egg yolks, salt and yeast mixture. Stir until smooth and dough leaves sides of bowl. Divide into 4 pieces and roll out as thin as possible; spread with filling. Place on greased pan and brush with egg white, very gently. Let stand in warm place for 1 hour. Bake at 350° for 30 minutes or until light brown. Cover with damp cloth as soon as it comes from the oven. Keep covered about 10 minutes to make a nice crust.

Directions for filling: Heat milk; add walnuts and stir. Add sugar, butter and lemon juice. Cool before spreading on dough.

Helen Horvath, *Fort Lauderdale, Florida*

"I'm afraid that's going to break the spell."

REIKO'S AUTHENTIC INDIAN CURRY

3 to 4 cups beef, pork, chicken or
  shrimp (raw or leftover)
Salt and pepper
2 or 3 large onions
2 cloves fresh garlic,
  finely chopped
2 to 3 tablespoons mild
  curry powder
10 tablespoons flour

4 or 5 carrots,
  cut into large chunks
1 large apple, grated
  (leave peel on)
2 small fresh tomatoes or
  1 can tomatoes
1 teaspoon fresh or
  ¼ teaspoon ground ginger

Brown meat well; salt and pepper. Sauté onions and garlic; add to meat; add curry powder and flour and sauté lightly. Add remaining ingredients plus about 4 cups water. Simmer gently all morning. Best when made early and served late. Serve over rice with such condiments as chutney, plumped raisins (soaked in boiling water 10 minutes), grated coconut, sliced bananas (sprinkled with orange juice), sliced apples (rinsed in a little water which is sprinkled with salt or pickle relish). Serves 8 to 10.

Ann Dingman, *Vienna, Virginia*

KARTOFFEL GLACE
(German Potato Balls)

9 large raw potatoes, grated
4 small cooked potatoes,
  grated or mashed
8 slices day-old bread, cubed
1 medium onion, grated
  (more if you wish)

1½ teaspoons salt
1 cup flour
1 teaspoon baking powder
2 tablespoons starch from potatoes
1 teaspoon chopped parsley
  (optional)

Cover grated raw potatoes with cold water while preparing other ingredients. Fry bread cubes in butter or margarine until dry and crisp. Drain raw potatoes and add to cooked potatoes, bread cubes, onion, salt, ½ cup flour, baking powder, starch from potatoes and parsley. Form into 2½-inch balls and roll in remaining ½ cup flour. Drop balls in boiling, salted water and cook gently approximately 20 minutes. Serve with pork or beef. Can be sliced when cold and fried in butter. Serves 8 to 10.

Mrs. Fred Slagle, *Rye, New York*

KUGEL
(Potato Casserole)

10 medium potatoes
1 small onion
1 teaspoon salt

Generous amount of garlic powder
¼ cup flour
2 tablespoons chicken fat

Chop potatoes and onions in blender. (Do one or two potatoes at a time, adding a little water each time. Then strain all.) Add all remaining ingredients: place in casserole and dot mixture with chicken fat. Bake, uncovered, for 1 hour at 400°. Cover casserole and bake a second hour at 350°. Serves 6.

Jennifer Gould, *Brighton, Massachusetts*

CHICKEN AND PORK MECHADA
(Philippine)

1 young chicken
  cut into regular pieces
1 pound lean pork, cubed
1 onion, diced
½ cup shortening
Salt and pepper
1 (15½-ounce) can tomato sauce

1 (8-ounce) can tomato paste
3 potatoes, quartered
3 carrots, quartered
½ red pepper, sliced
½ green pepper, sliced
1 can sweet peas
Rice

Sauté chicken, pork and onions in shortening in 6-quart Dutch oven. Season with salt and pepper. Add tomato sauce and tomato paste. Simmer for 10 minutes. Add potatoes, carrots and red and green peppers, and cook for 30 minutes or until meat is tender. Add sweet peas and simmer another 5 minutes. Serve with boiled rice, if desired. Serves 6.

Remy J. Garcia, *Peru, Indiana*

CAMARON REBOSADO
(Philippine Fried Shrimp)

1 pound shrimp
1 tablespoon salt
2 eggs
3 tablespoons flour

1 tablespoon cornstarch
1 teaspoon baking powder
Fat for frying

Sprinkle shrimp with salt and let stand for 1 hour. Beat eggs; add flour, cornstarch and baking powder. Mix thoroughly. Dip shrimp one at a time into batter and fry in deep fat.

Carmen Wilhelm, *Centreville, Virginia*

PIROZHKI
(Russian Meatballs)

Dough:

1 cake yeast (dissolved in ¼ cup water)	1 teaspoon salt
2 eggs	½ cup melted butter
1 tablespoon sugar	1 cup scalded milk
	3½ cups flour

Dissolve yeast in warm water. Let stand. In another bowl beat eggs. Then add everything to the yeast mixture—flour last. Turn out on floured board and knead until dough is soft and elastic. Place in lightly greased bowl and turn to grease top. Cover with cloth and place in warm area for 2 hours or until pastry doubles in bulk. Roll out and cut into 3-inch circles and fill with the following.

Filling:

2 pounds ground chuck	2 teaspoons salt
1 onion, chopped	3 or 4 dashes of pepper
1 tablespoon vegetable oil	1 hard-boiled egg, chopped

Sauté the above together until light brown. Put spoonful in middle of each pastry circle. Fold over and pinch together. Fry at 375° in deep fat for about 4 minutes, turning often. Drain on paper towels. Yield: approximately 2 dozen.

Mrs. Laurence Green, *Rolling Hills, California*

GREEK SPANAKOPITA
(Spinach-Cheese Pie)

¼ cup butter or margarine, melted	½ cup crumbled *feta* cheese or 3 tablespoons crumbled blue cheese
1 (8-ounce) can Italian flavored crescent dinner rolls, refrigerated	
3 eggs	2 cups finely chopped fresh spinach or 1 (10-ounce) package frozen, thawed, drained and chopped
1 (8-ounce) package cream cheese softened	
1 cup cottage cheese	

Pour 2 tablespoons butter over bottom of 13-by-9-inch baking pan. Separate crescent dough into 4 rectangles; place long sides of 2 rectangles together and press gently over bottom of prepared pan. Bake at 375°, 5 minutes. Meanwhile beat eggs lightly; add remaining ingredients and blend well, about 2 minutes. Pour over partially baked crust. Place long sides of remaining 2 rectangles together and roll into 13-by-9-inch rectangle; place over mixture in pan. With knife gently cut through top dough into serving portions. Bake at 375° for 30 minutes or until set and golden brown. Serve hot. Serves 12.

Mrs. Gus Daskalakis, *Salt Lake City, Utah*

INDEX

154